Charles Lee

A practical guide to the breeding, feeding, rearing & general management, for domestic use and exhibition of the Houdan fowl

Charles Lee

A practical guide to the breeding, feeding, rearing & general management, for domestic use and exhibition of the Houdan fowl

ISBN/EAN: 9783337147013

Printed in Europe, USA, Canada, Australia, Japan

Cover: Foto ©Lupo / pixelio.de

More available books at **www.hansebooks.com**

The Author's Houdan Cock "Lionel."
From a Photograph.

A PRACTICAL GUIDE

TO THE

BREEDING, FEEDING, REARING & GENERAL MANAGEMENT,

FOR DOMESTIC USE AND EXHIBITION,

OF

THE HOUDAN FOWL.

BY

CHARLES LEE.

LONDON:
PRINTED AND PUBLISHED BY W. HAWKINS, 3, ALBERT TERRACE, W.;
And by the Author,
21, WESTBOURNE GROVE, BAYSWATER, W.

1874.

ERRATA.

In page 10, line 4, for "common," read *commercial*.

In page 23, line 1, after "shape," insert the word *or*.

CONTENTS.

CHAPTER I.

THE ORIGIN OF THE HOUDAN, AND GENERAL OPINIONS RESPECTING THE BREED.

PAGE

Its origin. Merits of the breed and its characteristics, as allowed by various writers. Houdans *versus* Brahmas. Our first chickens. Points looked for in good specimens, &c. ... 9—24

CHAPTER II.

THE HOUDAN FROM AN ECONOMIC POINT OF VIEW, ITS CHARACTERISTICS, TREATMENT, &c.

Treatment in confined runs. How to utilize limited spaces. Egg-production. Plans for houses and yards. The system we adopted. Importance of cleanliness. Items in the economy of successful poultry-keeping. The proper period for hatching. Recipe for egg-producing. Laying stock, and how it should be selected. Precocity of the cockerels. The male birds as nurses. Practical management of stock. Drinking and feeding appliances. Overfeeding and its effects. Systematic feeding advocated. Remarks on the non-sitting instinct. The egg-producing trait, and how capable of being further improved. Value of the breed as table fowls. Early chickens. Economical method of feeding. Cost of chicken-rearing. Utility of the breed as a cross. Poultry-rearing under natural conditions. Moveable houses, &c. ... ... 25—64

CHAPTER III.

FATTENING. THE ENGLISH AND FRENCH SYSTEMS DESCRIBED. ITS RELATIVE VALUE IN A DOMESTIC AND COMMERCIAL SENSE.

Fattened and un-fattened chickens compared. The value of fattening for market purposes. A review of the English system. The French mode explained. Extra fattening. The cramming system. Feeding by machinery. Caponizing and poularde facturing. The art described. Treatment after the operation. Usefulness of capons, &c. ... ... 65—82

CONTENTS.

CHAPTER IV.
POULTRY-FANCYING, AND WHAT IT NECESSITATES.
PAGE

Amateurs and "professional" fanciers. Remarks on purchasing. Auctions and shows—their advantages and disadvantages. Commencing operations. Poultry honours, and questionable means of obtaining them. Disappointment from buying at random. Inferior and first-class chickens compared. Advantages of unrelated pens. Drawbacks of indiscriminate crossing. Stocking new yards. Points to be considered in mating. Size, crest, comb, colour, &c.—instructions for breeding for. Defects, and how capable of being remedied. The sex, how influenced by mating, &c. ... ... 83—100

CHAPTER V.
ON THE MANAGEMENT OF CHICKENS FOR EXHIBITIVE PURPOSES.

Eggs, their general appearance, and how they should be selected for hatching. Fertility, how easily ascertained. Disappointments in hatching, and how most frequently caused. Treatment during incubation. Hatching by artificial means. Hitherto supposed causes of failure. Results of our later experiments. The young broods. Coops. Early distinguishing signs of the sex. Appearance of the chicks when first hatched. Feeding. Means of attaining size. Feeding folds. Crooked breasts, and their preventative. Artificial mothers. Picking out waste chickens. Retarding laying. Advantages of medium-sized runs. Enemies to chickens. Means of ensuring early eggs, &c. ... ... 101—124

CHAPTER VI.
SUGGESTIONS ON EXHIBITING.

Special feeding. Selecting and matching. Points to be observed. Best plan to follow. Final treatment of the birds. Mr. Long on exhibiting. Treatment before and after showing. Characteristics of exhibitors. Scales for judging, &c. ... 125—137

CHAPTER VII.
WHITE HOUDANS.

White fowls and their admirers. Origin of the white variety. Appearance of the earlier specimens. Best plan for attaining size. Points to be cultivated. A correspondent's experience. How further success may be best attained. Scale for judging ... ... 138—149

INTRODUCTORY REMARKS.

We believe it was Max Schlesinger who once observed of prefaces, that they were mainly modest pleadings in which writers anticipating public censure, and well knowing how deserving they were of it, adduce various reasons why their books were not shorter or longer, and, in fact, altogether different, from the volumes which then and there are coupled with their names. For ourselves, if we are to plead guilty on any particular count, it ought, perhaps, to be for our temerity in appearing in print at all. But, seeing the oft-repeated enquiries in the leading poultry journals for information respecting one particular class of fowl, the Houdan, and being earnestly solicited by friends who were acquainted with our long practical study of the breed to pen the result of our observations, and thus give the public the benefit of our experience of its merits, we have at length overcome our personal scruples, and complied with their requests; not, however, without much diffidence, for we feel that we could with propriety and advantage to ourselves have left the discussion of the subject to far abler heads than ours; for it is easier by far to criticise the ideas of others than to advance opinions of one's own, and it, moreover, falls to the lot comparatively of but few men to be equal adepts with their pen and well acquainted with their subject. No practical writer being disposed to treat specially of this breed, we have ventured to pen the accompanying remarks, in the endeavour, as we have already intimated, to provide a want still existing amongst a certain class of poultry-keepers for information as to the culture of a breed of fowl whose merits have required no puffing to make it popular, both in the poultry-yard and on the table.

The Game, the Brahma, the Dorking, the Cochin, the Polish, the Spanish,—but why recapitulate them? suffice it that almost every other domestic variety has been ably represented by its respective admirers, and in one or more cases has formed the subject for an entire and special work. The fowl which has been the object of our study, and which forms the subject of the following pages, has been comparatively neglected. It has been *generally* described in lately-published poultry books, we admit, and a great many valuable observations of it have been recorded. But it has been treated rather as *one* of the French breeds instead of—in our opinion—*the most valuable of them all*. Whenever general notes are made of a group of varieties, it is next to impossible, however anxious and painstaking an author may be, to do full justice to a particular subject. In seeking, therefore, to supply this deficiency in poultry literature, we trust that we have not been too presumptuous in assuming that a small volume relating entirely to the Houdan will be acceptable.

In a report lately issued by the British Consul at Calais, relative to the supply of eggs from the French districts, and the introduction of French poultry for egg-production into this country, there is much valuable information. We gather from his remarks that the latter proceeding has not hitherto been attended with the degree of success anticipated; or, in other words, that, notwithstanding the productive alacrity displayed by French hens in certain parts of France, the results in England have not justified expectations founded upon it. Without attempting to question the alleged unproductiveness of French poultry generally, in our "tight little island," this cannot be said to apply to one type at least of Gaelic fowls, for "the Houdan" is not only particularly well adapted to the English climate, and a very formidable rival to our celebrated Dorking, but is not to be surpassed as an egg-producer by any other pure breed of fowl, if we judge it by, and *breed for, the useful qualities only*, as is done in France, instead of for the "fancy" points which, commercially, are of comparative inutility. Well may a writer in a daily paper * remark that we Britishers are very stupid egg-farmers; and that, although we can breed, with very few exceptions, the most splendid poultry to be found in the world, "we rear our Bantams, Cochin-Chinas, and Black Spanishers, &c., more with a 'fancying' than a commercial view; and display more ambition to take prizes at poultry shows than to enjoy cheap eggs and cheap fowls as food." The writer, moreover, points out that "the dairyman charges Londoners twopence halfpenny for a 'new-laid egg,' which is often a very 'ancient' affair; and a poulterer confidently asks five or six

---

* *Daily Telegraph*, Sept. 15th, 1874.

shillings for an attenuated chicken which a French *menagere* would think decidedly dear at two francs twenty-five centimes."

The report of the British Consul, to which we have previously alluded, would lead us to believe that a peculiarity of soil, such as is found in the *pas de Calais*, is essential to a large production of eggs. We believe this to be exaggerated; fowls must, of course, have some kind of grit with which to form the *shell* of the egg, and to keep them in health; but we feel assured that the success of French poultry is less dependent upon the ingredients of the soil than upon a *proper knowledge of the nature of the fowls*, and upon their *more general treatment*. If they are to give the maximum returns in egg-production, the habits and peculiarities of each distinct breed must be observed and studied, and the fowls must be fed and treated accordingly.

With the sole idea of guiding the poultry-keeper in this respect, we have penned the following pages—the result of close and careful study of the "one" breed to which we have for years specially devoted our attention. If an abundant supply of fine and fresh eggs is desired, the fowls must be kept with that view steadily before the eyes of their owner. If he wishes to have large and toothsome poultry, he will learn, we hope, how to procure such in the "Houdan Fowl." If his ambition points to exhibition fame, no worthier representative of poultry beauty can be seen than the fine antlered, crested, and bearded birds which are the subject of our book.

But the purpose for which the fowl is kept should be distinctly understood by the poultry-keeper. The Houdan is capable of realizing *either* of the just-named results for him, if treated consistently for the object desired; the mistake too frequently is made of treating the birds in the proper way for one purpose,— say, for instance, for exhibition, and expecting them at the same time to provide an abundant supply of eggs, or to be of great size and flavour on the table. Fowls, it must be always borne in mind, which are continually on the move from one exhibition to another, always kept more or less in "show form," are rarely fit for scarcely anything besides. Birds which are being fitted for the table are not those we should expect many eggs from; and genuine and abundant egg-producers are not the birds to have their necks broken or for competition in the show pen.

In compiling this little *brochure*, we may say at once that our aim throughout has been to be strictly practical rather than entirely original, and this announcement will possibly obviate not only the necessity of apologising for the various notes embodied, but answer any objection which may be made as to our pretensions for the task which we have, as we have already intimated, with the greatest diffidence undertaken. We have necessarily re-trodden portions of the well-worn track of some of our predecessors, but it is to be hoped that the results will justify the means. The correctness, too, of some of our views may possibly be questioned. We can only say that they are either the results of personal observation, of practical tests of other people's experience, or of information supplied to us by fanciers of this variety, on whose veracity we could entirely rely.

Apart from the many acts of assistance and advice which have been volunteered by esteemed friends and correspondents—and which would be but ill-requited on our part if we here omitted to tender our deepest obligations—reference has not unfrequently been made to "The Poultry Book" and "The Illustrated Book of Poultry," and we here take the opportunity of gratefully acknowledging to the respective and respected authors of both works many valuable suggestions. They have treated the general subject of Poultry and Poultry-keeping in a very elaborate manner; they have minutely described many details which it has been only necessary to touch more or less lightly in the following pages. Our object has been to treat of *one distinct breed*, and to avoid wearying the reader with everything which did not in some way directly or indirectly relate to it. How we have succeeded, our readers will be best capable of judging.

With all its faults—and we fear there are many—we now, however, commit our little work to the hands of those for whom it was specially written—the Amateur. If its perusal affords him but a tithe of the interest that the pleasure in compiling it involved on our part, we shall lay down our pen with satisfaction.

21, Westbourne Grove, Bayswater, W.,
October, 1874.

THE HOUDAN FOWL.

CHAPTER I.

THE ORIGIN OF THE HOUDAN, AND GENERAL OPINIONS RESPECTING THE BREED.

AMONGST the noisy kings and queens of the varied family of poultry, which year after year compete for distinction—and whose vocal efforts once heard at one of our leading shows are not easily forgotten—the French classes, it will not be denied, are presenting a fuller and better appearance; amongst them, as eminently conspicuous, we may enumerate the Houdan, and when it is taken into consideration the manifold *useful* qualities this fowl really possesses, its fast increasing popularity is not surprising.

Anterior to 1865 very little reliable information seems to have existed in this country respecting it, although a strong probability of its being not quite unknown some thirteen or fourteen years previous to this date seems apparent from a description (although a somewhat ambiguous one we admit), given by Messrs. Wingfield and Johnson in 1853, of a certain crested breed of fowl possessing not at all dissimilar characteristics to the one in question. Mention is certainly made at a more recent period, in more than one of the French poultry works, so far as can be gathered from the imperfect description there also given, of fowls which were famous for such individualities as are peculiar to the Houdan; but it was left to

B

Mr. Geyelin to first enlighten the English poultry community respecting its true appearance and utility, and which he did in 1865 in a pamphlet entitled " Poultry Breeding from a ~~Common~~ Point of View," as follows :—

" Whatever has been said to the contrary, this breed, when pure, is most characteristic; but it must be admitted that most of the farmers near Houdan know as little of the pure Houdan breed as those of La Fleche and Crêve-coeur know of theirs, and if you were to order some first-class breeds of them, irrespective of price, they would, with good conscience, forward fowls of a large size— but, from a want of knowledge, some cross breeds. To illustrate this, I may mention that I could have purchased at the markets in those localities splendid thorough-bred specimens for about three shillings—the price of common fowls—but which were worth in France even a pound each. There are, however, in each locality some persons who take an interest in their pure breeds, particularly since they have been encouraged by the reward of prizes from poultry exhibitions.

" The Houdan fowl has a very bulky appearance, its plumage invariably black and white spangled, a crest of the same color, comb triple, the outsides opening like two leaves of a book, and the centre having the appearance of an ill-shaped long strawberry. With the cock the comb is very large, whilst with the hen it ought to be scarcely perceptible. The legs are strong and of a lead colour, with five claws, the two hind ones being above the others. Strongly developed whiskers both in the cocks and hens. This is one of the finest races of fowls, but its qualities surpass even its beauties. Besides the smallness of their bones and the fineness of their flesh, they are of an extraordinary precocity and fecundity; they lay large white eggs, and the chickens are fit for the table at four months old. The weight of adults is from seven to eight pounds, in which the bones figure for one-eighth. The chickens, when four months old, weigh, without the intestines, about four and a half pounds."

Respecting its origin, little is really known; the principal market town of Nantes in the southern part of France, called Houdan, where a brisk poultry traffic was, and we believe is still carried on, has probably been instrumental for the appelation the fowl now bears. But we apprehend that neither it or indeed any other variety of the French type can fairly claim more title to distinctness of species than some of the different classes of Bantams can be said to do, and which it is scarcely necessary to observe are merely varieties of a domesticated kind which by repeated crosses and careful breeding have been brought to their present state of perfection by man's careful art, and certainly present one of the most forcible and triumphant examples of what may be accomplished when skill and judgment, seconded by patience and perseverance, are brought to bear upon a subject.

Our light-hearted friends in the French provinces have in a similar manner, but to a different end, directed their energies to the improvement of the more useful qualities of their home-feathered stock, thereby showing us how other valuable results may be achieved, for it can now scarcely be questioned that nearly all, if not the whole, of their different varities have been really formed by making choice of fowls famous for certain special individual qualities, crossing these gradually with other fowls of a different breed, but likewise excelling in characteristics equally valuable, upon these again, grafting others of a tantamount value, until they have at last succeeded, in course of years, in producing such specimens of a poulterer's handicraft as cannot possibly be surpassed in *economic* worth by any *pure* breed of fowl we possess.

It has been suggested that the Poland and the Dorking have at some former period, and by such a system as we have enumerated, been the principal and original sources of the Houdan's formation and the grounds for such an hypothesis are more than slight, notwithstanding we have seen it asserted that the Dorking and the Houdan have nothing in common. The plea that the colour of the legs and plumage and the non-sitting instinct as being sufficient to confirm such an assertion, appears to us to be no answer whatever, for it is so well known that in breeding, most features and propensities can be, by studied attention more clearly defined, improved, or so diverted from their original source as to leave scarcely a trace; and in making these remarks we must not overlook the probable fact that both the Polish and the Dorking are also in *their* turn merely the offspring of mixed breeds.

If, however, we accept the theory of a Polish foundation as a correct one, we are at no loss in arriving at the probable source of the crest and muffling, the cavernous nostrils, the wonderful laying instinct, the delicious and juicy flesh, and and the very rare desire the Houdan evinces for incubation. Again, in size and form the type so very closely approaches that of our famous Dorking, that the idea of the blood of the latter having been instrumental in its production is also worth considering, for the deep, square, compact frame offers in this respect strong indications. The readiest solution, too, for the fifth toe which to our minds is really the only objectionable feature in the Houdan, is in this manner more readily to be accounted for. But previous to dismissing this portion of our subject, we perhaps cannot do better than quote the remarks of two able authorities, viz., Mr. Tegetmier, and Mr. Wright, respecting the opinions we have given. The former gentleman in his masterly work, "The Poultry Book," in page 92, speaking of the Dorking, and negativing the supposition of its being descended from the Roman fowls, makes the following significant remark.—" It is singular that the

English table-fowl, the Dorking, and the French table-fowls, the Crève-cœur and the Houdan, should be, as they evidently are, composite breeds, perfected in a long series of years, during which time the sole object of the rearers has been to obtain a first-class table fowl by breeding from any birds whose form and size was likely to improve the original stock." The probability of a cross at some remote period between the Dorking and the Silver Padoue, or some other variety of the Polish breed, is also spoken of by Mr. Wright in "The Practical Poultry Keeper," page 166, for speaking of the Houdan he there states "This fowl in many respects resembles the Dorking, and Dorking blood has evidently assisted at its formation. We believe that a cross between the latter and a White Poland would not be very wide of the mark." Again, in his more recent and elaborate work, "The Illustrated Book of Poultry," page 410, after alluding to the "one point in common," all the French breeds possess of delicious flavour, he gives it as his opinion that Houdans "moreover show in a very suggestive manner what may be done by a judicious selection in the way of founding new breeds, since they are evidently built upon the Polish foundation, obtaining from this race the juicy flesh, excellent laying qualities, and absence of incubating instinct, whilst size has been added from foreign sources."

If further arguments were necessary respecting the certainty of the Houdan being a "manufactured race," it would be best answered, we venture to think, by pointing out the great *uncertainty* which existed until quite recently of the extra toe, or the crest, or muffling, being reproduced in breeding. For it frequently occurred that full-crested, well-muffled birds threw offspring without a particle of these appendages, whilst four-toed chickens were also produced when both parents were in full possession of the objectionable, but in a "fancy" sense, necessary "fifth." Scientific breeding has happily rendered these drawbacks less conspicuous than formerly, and the Houdan, *if properly mated*, now breeds very true to character. Still as the deviations we have pointed out are not yet extinct, the fact would seem to considerably strengthen the arguments we have adduced.

Since Mr. Geyelin's description of the breed first appeared, there has been no want of contributaries to testify to the alleged value of the Houdan, and of the many who have thus given publicity to their experience, it may not perhaps be unadvisable if we briefly quote a few remarks from one or two well-known writers whose authority and testimony will not be questioned. In so doing (and previous to recording our own experience) the reader will have an opportunity of observing how far the results of the last few years has justified Mr. Geyelin's original observations.

The following opinions respecting the merits of the breed are thus given by Mr. F. Zurhorst, of Dublin, and are thus recorded in Mr. Tegetmier's Poultry Book:—

"I do not hesitate to commence with the broad assertion that they are by far the most valuable breed that has been added to our collection for many years. Unusual fertility: I never knew an egg fairly set to miss; very early maturity, extreme hardiness, both as adults and chickens, together with a large compact Dorking body, with little offal, white flesh, and legs only slightly shaded, are the leading characteristics of the breed. Abundant layers of moderate-sized eggs, they in this point far excel the Crêve-coeurs, which are only moderate in this respect, and their broken plumage of black and white, handsome crests, and branching coral combs, make them fully their equals in beauty. As a cross with our common breeds they are of inestimable value, not only from the certainty of the introduction of thoroughly alien blood, but also from the valuable characteristics I have named.

"The abominable fifth claw, which I suppose must be insisted on as a mark of purity of the breed, is by no means a certainty, as many chickens come out four-clawed, and would not be difficult to breed out; but I must say, as far as my observation extends, it has not in this breed the detrimental effect it has on our highly-bred Dorkings, much of whose tendency to disease of the foot and claw I attribute to this monstrosity."

We wish we could endorse the correctness of Mr. Zurhorst's opinion regarding the exemption of the Houdan in this respect, but time has not substantiated it, for it is but too evident that since the establishment of the fifth toe has become absolute, the consequences he speaks of are still on the increase, and although writer follows writer in deprecating the inevitable evils thus produced, this in every sense useless feature is firmly maintained.

Following the writer we have just quoted, we have at a more recent date the experienced remarks of an authoress of no mean pretentions—viz., the Hon. Mrs. Arbuthnot—better, perhaps, known to poultry cultivators as Mrs. Fergusson Blair, who thus sums up their value in her admirable little work, "The Hen Wife":—

"I gladly repeat my testimony as to the superior qualities of some of the French breeds, especially the Houdan, whether viewed as table or merely ornamental poultry. My experience has been acquired principally in Scotland; therefore, if any birds thrive in this cold and often damp climate, they ought to do even better in more favoured quarters. The Houdan is very hardy, and can live anywhere; they eat little, moult with ease, and are precocious layers. Pullets hatched in May are laying in October, and if their eggs were set at once, the produce would bring large prices as spring chickens in March. I have it much at heart to introduce these ' model hens ' into our farm-yards, and make them *par excellence* the farm-yard bird. The Houdans are well known and sufficiently appreciated in France, where they rival, and many think excel, the better-known Crêve-coeur and La Fleche breeds; I acknowledge the merits of these, but claim a higher place for the Houdans as a hardier race and of faster growth than either of the others. They lay large, beautifully-formed white eggs, which, like the diminutive Hamburg, seldom fail in hatching. I have kept Houdans in great numbers, and never have had a badly-formed egg from them; the chickens grow and feather rapidly, and nothing can be better as table poultry—added to which they are very ornamental. They sometimes show a desire to incubate, but their *forte* lies in laying; therefore I strongly recommend their being kept as the egg-suppliers of the establishment, and am not afraid, if once tried, of any adverse opinion."

Mr. R. B. Wood, again, thus writes in "The Illustrated Book of Poultry," page 411:—" I have now kept Houdans for nearly seven years, and can safely say that I have not found them fall off in any way, but quite the contrary. I find them good layers of fine eggs, and as table fowls not, in my opinion, to be surpassed. They are very hardy as chickens, feathering and maturing in a much shorter time than either Brahmas or Cochins. I consider them a very valuable breed for any one to keep when non-sitters are required, as it is very rare for them to show the least tendency to incubate. It is also worthy of remark that though good foragers when at liberty, they are easily kept in bounds, being very different to the Hamburgs or Game in this respect, and they will bear confinement as well as most breeds."

The talented author of the work from which we have just

quoted moreover observes : " We never reared any (Houdans) ourselves but once, some years ago, when we hatched a sitting of eggs sent by rail. We found these chicks hardier even than our Brahmas, and they appeared to feather as if by magic; but being from a small and recently-imported strain, did not make much weight by the time they were killed."

So far, then, it will be seen that Mr. Geyelin's first impression of the breed is not suggestive of any want of confirmation; but, on the contrary, succeeding writers have only strengthened it. But as the proprietor of the "Bazaar" kindly gave insertion to many letters of a controversial nature during the year of 1873 respecting the Brahma and the Houdan, we select the following three letters as bearing more immediately upon the point at issue. Although we can ourselves readily testify as to the many merits of our "feathered-legged friends," the controversy nevertheless afforded us no little pleasant satisfaction in noticing how rapidly the Houdan was then gaining in the number of its supporters.

One writer, who assumes the *nom de plume* of "Cowbow," says : " Houdans lay so very well, and there is really so little trouble required with them, that I prefer them to the Brahmas; they are hardy, and never worry any one with their sitting propensities. They also lay as well as the Brahmas during the winter, and commence earlier. I hatched some last year in July, and they began to lay a fortnight before Christmas, and continued until last month, when they began to moult. I do not pretend to say they have all laid every day throughout that time, but I only had six hens of that breed, and I had Houdan eggs nearly (if not quite) every day during the first eight and a half months of this year. The size of the Houdan may be increased if less attention were paid to fancy points."

The following is from the pen of "An amateur who has made poultry keeping pay," and if any of our readers should feel disposed to take an incredulous view of some of the statements therein contained, we may observe that they are not at all at variance with the result which we ourselves have attained. The writer says:—"I have kept poultry now for some time, including Brahmas, Spanish, Cochins, and Houdans, and have long ago arrived at the conclusion that Houdans "bear the palm." As an instance of this, in the last week of Dec., 1871, ten of my own Houdan pullets "came into profit," and from that time until the commencement of October, of the present year, viz., forty-one weeks, when moulting began, I never got less than thirty eggs per week, but, generally speaking, forty, forty-five, or fifty, but, at all events, making from the beginning to the termination of their laying season the large number of 1637 eggs. Of course, good feeding has been my *forte*. I have tried the above-named breeds, but never could produce anything like the above results I have with Houdans; I have found that Cochins and Brahmas, aye, and Spanish, too, are all enormous eaters. Now my Houdans eat very little more than half the same quantity of food, and give me back the greater proportion of it in the shape of good-sized and delicate-flavoured eggs. I say again, for profitable fowls commend me to Houdans. I have heard they have drawbacks, but I cannot certainly say I have experienced any. On the contrary, I maintain they are more hardy, precocious, productive, and profitable, taking them all the year round, than any other breeds I am acquainted with. Crêves are being highly extolled just now; but will they bear comparison with Houdans in any of the above, after providing for their enormous appetites and taking the number and weight of a batch of eggs laid throughout the season by each fowl respectively?

When I state that my yard is only 30ft. by 55ft., it will be seen that those who have larger spaces at command should have no trouble in doing what I have done; but, at all events, it contradicts the popular error that Houdans 'cannot be kept in confinement.'"

We give one more illustration as showing the precocity of Houdans, and the small amount of care needed to make them profitable, which we take from the same source as the preceding. This correspondent remarks, "I have two friends, small poultry fanciers, who keep—the one Brahmas, the other Houdans; he of the Brahmas had a brood in March and more in June, while there were no Houdans hatched till the middle of July. My friends had great success with the chickens nearly all coming to maturity; but although so much older than the Houdans, the first hatch of Brahmas did not lay a fortnight before them, whilst the second lot of Brahmas were at least a month behind the Houdans. Both lots were fed on about the same kind of food, but the Brahmas had more of it. The Brahmas had an unlimited grass run, while the Houdans had no more than a few yards of bare earth, with a cabbage now and then. As to the marketable value of the birds, Houdans are greatly preferred to Brahmas, as I have myself ascertained. I had a few Brahma cockerels to dispose of, so sent them to market with some young Houdans, which although much smaller, fetched more than the others, a great deal. To anyone wanting a good hardy fowl that lays well, and makes a decent appearance on the table, I say, "keep Houdans."

In thus reviewing the foregoing opinions as to the general merits of Houdans, we gather the following, then, as being admitted facts. Their noble and distinguished appearance, astonishing hardihood, unprecedented precociousness, both as to growth and laying instincts, good quality of flesh, unusual fertility of their eggs, facility with which the chickens can be reared, their value as market fowl, and their usefulness in crossing, and thereby improving other breeds.

Our first personal knowledge of the Houdan was in the spring of 1865, when a friend on business in Paris brought over with him on his return a pen of fowls which had, it appeared, struck his fancy as being somewhat "peculiar," and which he had purchased (to what seemed to us then) for the extravagant price of sixty-six francs. Although presenting the general Houdan type, they were, we can very well recollect, a very different class of fowl compared to what modern breeding has engendered. They stood high upon the leg, the cock bird particularly so, whilst the general groundwork of the plumage was a dirty white, irregularly splashed with brownish-black spots, but of an entirely lustreless hue, and with an abundance of yellow feathers in the hackles. The cock weighed, to the best of our recollection, something over 8lbs. and his two consorts about a pound each less. Most grotesque looking bipeds we thought them, with their large top-knots and strange looking combs and whiskers; but they established themselves favourites from the onset by the tame and happy-tempered disposition they evinced by eating out of any body's hand with the greatest *sang froid* imaginable, and also submitting to be stroked and handled by our friend's children as quietly as a cat or dog.

From the first day we saw them we took a considerable amount of interest in these fowls, and studied their characteristics, as far as we possibly could do, on every occasion; but the following February of 1866, when a sitting of ten eggs, which had been presented to us by our friend, produced to our unexpected delight nine lively chicks (for the season, it may be recollected, was a severe one), our interest became redoubled, and although the accommodation at our disposal was then of the most limited character, we, in the face of that and other difficulties, nevertheless succeeded in bringing up every one of our interesting *protegees*, and which on the good, though plain, yet liberal feeding we gave them, matured so very fast that at the early part of the following August the pullets (five in number) began to fill our egg basket very rapidly, they being at this time, it must be recollected, not quite five months and a half old. The cockerels grew into splendid birds—we mean in point of size; but the pullets in this respect showed a very considerable falling off as compared to the mother hens. In those days, however, we had plenty to learn, and never gave a thought to the fact that " very early laying was prejudicial to size;" but we were fully satisfied with the results, and as year by year since then, with the aid of occasional importations and a due regard to mating, feeding, &c., acquired from a practical study of the breed, we have had no occasion to alter our earlier-formed opinion that "the Houdan was bound to become a very popular fowl." How far this opinion was justified we will leave the reader to deduce his own conclusions.

But in dismissing these reminiscences of our earlier experience, and before discussing the general management of the breed, it may be as well to describe those points which characterize good birds.

A Houdan cock fully grown, and with any pretentions to prize-winning in good company, should not in weight be less than eight or nine pounds, although this is at times exceeded the last mentioned may be considered as good; but as this is really one of the most important features in the breed, we need scarcely say that "size" should be sedulously cultivated. In form, the body should present a particularly full and square appearance, the shoulders, saddle, and back being very wide, the latter drooping slightly towards the tail, whilst the breast should be also conspicuous for breadth and fulness; the wings carried well up, but properly developed.

The colour of the plumage should show, as far as possible, a uniformity of black and white,—that is to say a splashing of these two colours, as evenly distributed throughout as possible, but on the breast particularly. In speaking of the black, we do not mean that "dead" black which at one time was but too prevalent, but one of a vivid greenish olive tint. Although in accordance with modern requirements, we have bred the dark variety now all the rage (but not *quite* so dark, we may observe, as our bird "Lionel" is depicted in the frontispiece) we nevertheless incline towards much lighter coloured birds for show purposes ourselves, as being more in accordance with what Houdans *should* be. Dark ones we freely admit, on one side or the other, are undoubtedly better adapted for breeding purposes, owing to the tendency this fowl has to get lighter after each successive moult; but we cannot at all reconcile ourselves to the belief that birds almost black (as now shown) are best entitled to prize-taking.

The head should be surmounted by a large, well-arched, but full tuft of feathers, known as the top-knot or crest, composed of long and narrow plumage, falling well back so as to leave the comb fully exposed; but the face itself, which should be red, is greatly hidden by feathers also, encircling it and the throat, in the form of whiskers; and in all good specimens there is, moreover, a well-defined bunch of these feathers depending from the under part of the beak, and known as the beard, which altogether give a particularly grotesque appearance to the bird. The spiral comb which has of late been so much in vogue, we consider altogether a mistake, and no doubt is the resulting effects of crosses with the Crêvecoeur, for the production of the dark coloured birds which we have already observed are now so prevalent at our leading shows. The two-leaved comb, or more correctly speaking, the antlered shape, as described by Mr. Geyelin, viz., "a triple comb with the outsides opening like two leaves of a book, and having the appearance of an ill-shaped strawberry in the centre, is a prominent point breeders should maintain, for the Houdan comb proper ought to be as distinctive in character from that of the Crêve as can well be imagined. If this is neglected, and these "dark gems" are in future to be the only prize-takers, the Houdan will gradually merge into a spotted Crêve.

The growth of red skin from the lower mandables of the beak, termed wattles, should be moderately long, rather thin, but particularly red, assimilating in the latter condition to the comb. The nostrils should have a particularly wide and cavernous appearance, the beak be very strong and rather dark in colour, and the eyes of a bright and restless character. From the neck and saddle, elongated narrow pointed feathers, resembling in shape those of the crest,—but of a darker and and more lustrous hue, interspersed with white, and commonly known respectively, as the neck and saddle hackles, should be conspicuous and full, long, and sweeping, which greatly enhances the general appearance.

Red and straw-coloured feathers in the hackles were formerly prevalent in most of the cock birds, but good breeding has at length overcome this, and any indication of the former in a show bird would now be an objection of a fatal character. But we must observe that a straw-coloured or yellowish tinge is very frequently acquired both in the crest and hackles of a Houdan cock, *as he gets older,* but which we have in no way found detrimental to breeding. The tail should be very full, carried nearly erect, be well sickled and of a lustrous greenish black hue; The thighs and legs, in some strains have been to our thinking a little too long; but this is getting better. Moderately thick, but short, should be the pattern, and of a white or pinky-white tint, very slightly, if at all, mottled, and free from feathers. The toes should be well-formed and straight, but the fifth toe should be quite distinct, well developed and curved upwards. There is a proud, upright, yet lively bearing in the deportment of the bird, not easy to describe, but particularly striking.

In the hen, a fair average exhibition weight may be estimated as about six and a half to seven and a half pounds, although in breeding for weight alone we have considerably added to this. She should resemble the cock bird in general characteristics, excepting that her crest, comb, and wattles vary in shape and size, and the markings, in her case, should be altogether of a smaller and more defined character. But our idea of what a first-class Houdan hen ought to be will be gathered from the following:

"We should in the first place look for a full, square-bodied bird of fair size, with broad straight back, well-proportioned tail, the latter not carried too high. Her crest very full, round, compact, and evenly marked: her comb resembling that of the cock, in shape and colour, but very small. Nicely formed whiskers should join the crest and beard, and slightly hide the eyes and ear lobes. The beard we would prefer of a bell-shaped form depending rather loosely from the beak; the latter dark, as in the male bird; and her hackles full of evenly-marked feathers. Nice short, but stoutish shanks, and legs of a light colour should support her body, her claws being all well formed, and the fifth claw in particular well grown, curved upwards, and quite distinctive from the others. Such points as these, united to general uniformity of marking, are not every day to be met with, and such a bird as we have thus described naturally would not fail to carry off the highest prize, in almost the sharpest competition."

Fig. 1.

HOUSE AND RUN SUITABLE FOR A LIMITED SPACE.

Missing Page

Missing Page

possible occasion. To keep out the excessive heat in summer, or retain warmth in the winter months, a light frame of oiled canvas can, when desired, be placed across a portion of the front, and will answer these ends without excluding too much light. But situation need not be so much studied in this breed, as is really necessary in the case of delicate varieties, for as regards the hardihood of Houdans we can say from experience that neither as chickens or adults can they in this respect be surpassed. It must not, however, be inferred that this breed can thrive in the face of *every* drawback (although we have known them do so in a great many) any more than any other class of fowl, and unless a due amount of attention be paid to certain requirements which in *confinement* is absolutely necessary to their welfare, profitable results can scarcely be expected. All fowls in close confinement have not been inaptly compared to the diver whilst pursuing his avocation under fathoms of water; both certainly are but "artificial" means of existence, to say the least, and precisely as the diver supports life by a continuous supply of fresh air from above, so must fowls have those requisites they would procure for themselves if at liberty. Therefore grass, or other green vegetable food, lime, grit, or gravel, and a substitute for their natural worm and insect food, they must have. This is readily effected by making a "heap" at one end of the "run," of earth, grit, and bricklayer's rubbish, say, about a bushel of each, with a few large sods of grass, with plenty of the earth adhering piled on the top; these sods should be given daily if possible, the other ingredients will last for a long time. Thus employment—which is of more importance to fowls than is frequently supposed—and a certain amount of food are provided at the same time; they will soon level the heap in their search for treasures, but it should be piled up again every morning, all droppings being first removed. Most fowls will do well under these conditions—Houdans particularly so—if cleanliness and attention to their trifling wants and comforts be studied. In a state of confinement, which is far from natural to them, never let it be forgotten, they are kept for the pleasure or profit of the owner, and it should therefore be a matter of duty, as well as interest, that they are properly cared for.

Where eggs and chickens too are wished for, accommodation of a much larger extent than the foregoing will be a matter of necessity. It is not, however, meant to be implied that adults cannot be well kept, and chickens also reared successfully, unless they have an extensive range, although many writers have certainly ridiculed the idea of bringing up chickens unless in this manner. Such a supposition, however, is not only inaccurate, but even absurd, for, whilst fully admitting the superior advantages of fresh air and green fields, we have known so many instances where aspiring amateurs have shown such an amount of zest for the pursuit, that they have not only reared their young stock under the most surprising and unheard-of disadvantages, but have done so so successfully that they have carried off prizes from birds born and bred in a far more natural manner. The point, then, to be borne in mind is, that where fowls are to be kept, or chickens reared, in comparative confinement, their wants *must* be supplied as closely to nature as their owner's circumstances will admit. The space, then, to be set apart, if really of a restrictive kind, should however still be large enough to allow for at least two distinct houses and runs for separating the adult stock from the chickens, and a plot of grass, or well-gravelled ground—however small it may be—for rearing the latter.

In suggesting how this may be done both economically and satisfactorily, and also as affording another instance of how not only full-grown fowls can be kept in health and con-

GROUND PLAN.

```
         | a |                    B                      | a |
     b   | b |              Covered Run.                  | b |
     A   | A |                                            | A |
     d   | d |  c           d              c              | d |
```

C
Open Run.
d

Covered Run.   D   Covered Run.
              d Gravelled Yard.   d

B   B

Scale.
1   5   10   15   20   25   30

A A Roosting and Laying Houses.	a a Nests.
B B Covered Runs.	b b Perches.
C Open Run.	c c Holes for Fowls to enter.
D Gravel Yard.	d d Doors.

(Fig. 2.)

dition, but chickens be raised also, in moderate numbers, on a piece of ground of very small extent, *providing due care be only taken*, we have briefly sketched the outlines of our own procedure and have given in Fig. 2 the ground-plan of our original home-yard. This was at one time our sole resource for supplying (on a very inadequate scale, it is true) the growing demand for eggs and chickens which has now necessitated more ample accommodation, for we see no reason for disguising the fact that our recreation has been no less a profitable than a pleasing one. As will be seen from this plan, the space at command comprised an area of only thirty feet wide by about the same in length, if we except an additional storey we had afterwards built; and on this comparatively small piece of ground we used frequently to rear to maturity from seventeen to five and twenty of our Houdan chicks yearly—of a healthy and choice kind, too, and which realized very satisfactory sums when disposed of. The three covered runs were made weather proof and wired in with inch-and-a-half galvanized wire-netting, on the sides communicating with the open yard, on the same principle as already recommended for fig. 1. It will be perceived that each run had a separate house for the chickens and adult fowls to roost and lay in, and that communication with the whole, when necessary, was easily effected by opening a door or lifting a trap. The yard, we may observe, was shared at intervals, in fine weather, alternately between the occupants of the two side runs. In these latter our chickens were fed and allowed to run loose in the open yard in very dry weather only. The back run was reserved for our breeding stock; our hens were mostly set in some snug and convenient corner within our own dwelling, and we always made it our endeavour to set two or more hens at the same period, when we were fortunate enough to get them broody. For this purpose we preferred smallish-sized Brahmas or Cochins, and as soon as the little ones were hatched, to let one hen take charge of two broods, and set the other again with some fresh eggs — we thus economised both time and space. The system of feeding we adopted will have due attention hereafter. When our chickens had attained the age of eight weeks, we separated the pullets from the cockerels. Arrived at the age of twelve weeks, or sometimes even less, our plan was to make a due inspection of the whole lot, removing the inferior ones, mostly for domestic use. By these means we generally had in hand a moderate stock of promising young birds, and by thus continuing to repeat this "weeding out" process, those that we preserved were, if only few in number, certainly superior in quality. The ground in our covered runs being of a very clayey nature, we had it dug out to the depth of a foot and a half and filled in with concrete, and upon this fine earth, lime rubbish, roadside grit, and gravel in equal proportions to about the same depth was strewn upon it, and which we raked over every morning ourselves; about once a fortnight we had all of it sifted, removing the droppings, and the whole was replenished with fresh material as often as we thought it necessary. In fact, what we wanted in space we made up by cleanliness, and thus kept our yard free from disease. When we borrowed strange hens, as we were always then compelled to do, they were duly examined before we put any eggs under them to make sure they were not troubled by vermin. They thus set closer and more steadily, and we had better broods. During the prevalence of summer heats, we further made a point of sprinkling the floors of the houses and perches with a solution of disinfecting powder, which not only kept the habitations cool and sweet, but certainly tended to free them from parasites, to the comfort of the occupants. The laying nests, which were simply formed of two strips of wood partitioned off, were replenished with fresh straw before they were allowed to get musty, and every part of them, also the interior of the houses and walls of the runs, were washed over well, twice or thrice a year, with hot lime and water, which not only gave them a cleanly appearance, but really made them so. Our success, then, it will be seen, was really achieved by the strictest observance of cleanliness and system. "Work" and "trouble" were words in our vocabulary, the meaning of which we never fully understood in their relation to the poultry-yard—hence the result. Further details of our general management we need not here particularize, as they will be found in various portions of the work; but having learnt the importance of cleanliness and sweetness in every department of chicken-rearing ourselves, particularly with limited accommodation, we cannot but advise our readers to attend strictly to these apparently minor details, but details, however, on which mainly depend the *healthful success of the undertaking*.

Respecting the profitability, of the Houdan in a domestic sense only, and under such conditions as we have been discussing, the result must be said to depend chiefly upon the amateur himself, for in nine instances out of every ten the pursuit is really undertaken without the least regard to "system;" and unless such is brought into requisition, no breed of fowl can be expected to produce results of a very satisfactory kind.

Amongst some of the items in the economy of poultry-keeping a most important (and frequently neglected one) is a due attention to the age of the laying stock. The latter should be composed of February, March, or April-hatched pullets, a corresponding number hatched in the same months of the preceding year; and a like proportion of two-year-old hens in addition, and the best rule in the matter is, on no consideration to keep any of the stock after their third autumn, * when required simply for laying purposes; for many as may be the eggs a Houdan pullet will lay during her first season, such will bear no comparison, either in size or in number, to that of the *following* one; and although we have had instances where this *has* been equalled the succeeding year, it certainly must be regarded as an exception. Not unlike certain other breeds, the *second* season of the Houdan must be looked on as the most profitable if considered simply as a layer. But to realize the fullest modicum of profit in every way, immediately a hen discontinues to add to the egg-basket as her third autumn approaches, and directly any indication of moulting is noticed, either the knife, or other means, should terminate her existence without delay; two years and a half will generally be found the most appropriate period; the flesh, although of course not possessing the delicate juicy flavour of a cockerel or pullet, will nevertheless be in good eatable condition at this age with or without fattening; but if the fowl is kept longer than the period mentioned, the egg returns will decrease, and the carcase be only fit for boiling down to make "stock."

The next question for consideration is perhaps the best period for hatching, and herein possibly depends the whole result of whether the rearing and keeping of any class of fowl be a loss or a gain; for the time of year in which chickens are hatched determines whether the pullets will finally pay for their rearing. It will very naturally have been assumed, by many of our readers, from some of our own and previous writers' observations, that Houdan pullets, under all circum-

---

* In the question of prize poultry this will not apply, for very frequently the value of a setting of eggs from one hen will be more than an equivilent for many months of feeding, to say nothing of her qualities in a prize-taking sense.

stances and conditions, will begin to lay at the age we have previously specified, namely, between their fifth and sixth month. This, however, will give rise to disappointment, unless the period when they are hatched be systematically regulated. Let us take, for instance, the case of birds hatched in May, and what month in the whole year presents more favourable advantages *apparently* than this? but in spite of all the good feeding, it will frequently happen that Christmas festivities are in full swing before the pullets begin to lay. Those hatched a month later, or during June, will do even worse, for in this instance it is not at all uncommon for March to arrive—the pullets being thus nine months old—ere any profit is returned for the food expended.

The great question, then, of "how to make this branch of poultry-keeping profitable," hangs mainly on *early hatching* and *appropriate feeding*. Chickens hatched at the latter end of February or March, or the commencement of April, will necessarily give more trouble than those hatched in May, but they will repay that trouble threefold, whereas the later-hatched birds will almost prove a dead loss. We all know that fowls lay more or less freely in summer, but that is not the thing. The grand "paying" question is, to have them laying in winter, when every egg represents " money," and consequent profit, and winter-laying fowls are to be obtained only by the special rule we have advocated, bearing in mind that no pullet hatched after April will ever bear a *real* profit to her keeper.*

---

* Mr. Wright has pointed out these facts very forcibly in the "Illustrated Book of Poultry," page 21. He there says, "Supposing that the average time for a pullet to commence laying is at the age of six months, and that the cost of her food be—as in large breeds it is—about three halfpence per week, a late May pullet must be fed three months longer, at an additional outlay of one shilling and sixpence, before she yields any return. No fowl—we speak

By having the stock of different ages as already pointed out, there will thus be a certainty of not only having a fair average of eggs during the winter months, but also of having some portion of the stock always ready for domestic requirements, inasmuch as each autumn the fowls which have just attained their two and a half year will be killed, and there places filled up by the pullets, which August or September should find laying, and which ought to continue laying throughout the winter, if moderately well fed. By the time these leave off, or very frequently before, the year-old hens will have completed their moult, and will contribute their moiety also to the egg basket. This is the only way a continuous supply of eggs can be ensured, either in large or small poultry yards.

We need scarcely state that any diet of a forcing or stimulating character will promote laying at an earlier period than that of an opposite kind; therefore, the following recipe "for making pullets lay at five months old," which was advertised rather extensively a year or so ago in some of the poultry journals, although not by any means containing any startling information, may nevertheless, as the writer remarks "be useful to all who are interested in poultry, and

---

now of mere ordinary or market stock, not of fancy values—can be expected to recover such a cost; and it is in this way that about half the failures in poultry-keeping are caused. Ordinary fowls become broody oftener in May than any other month, and the bright warm days tempt the proprietor to choose that time for hatching the chickens. The latter do well, indeed they enjoy themselves and thrive and grow, but they will not pay, whereas chickens hatched from the middle to the end of March, or early in April, will require more attention certainly, and call for much self-denial occasionally, in the shape of braving bad weather, to see they are duly cared for; but will oftener, if in reach of a town market, repay the whole of their cost even before the New Year."

who also wish an abundant supply of eggs." In furtherance of this end, we therefore quote it *in extenso* :—

"The chief thing I have found, and also the best for egg-producing is malt. I always give my fowls malt from chickenhood, and I have found by experience that by its use they grow fast, and generally lay in five months. I change the food as often as I possibly can, but never allow one day to pass but that they have malt; the quantity I give is two handfulls for every six fowls daily. I generally mix it with the soft food, which is composed of boiled potatoes or peelings, barley flour, Indian meal, and bran. I have found by experience that it is best to give soft food for the first meal. If the weather be cold, I season the soft food with pepper and salt, and sometimes mix it with ale or beer. Twice a week I boil a sheep's bag or bullock's liver, chopped fine, and mix with the soft food—quantity, quarter pound to each fowl. The second meal I sometimes give soft food, and sometimes corn. I always give corn for the last meal, such as barley, Indian corn, and oats mixed, and during the moulting time I mix with the corn hempseed, say one handful to each fowl daily. I always change the water twice a day, and in winter add to the water a few drops of solution of sulphate of iron, just enough to give a slight mineral taste. I always take care that they are fed regularly, and never allowed more than what they can eat at a time."

The *rationale* of the above treatment, which we may add may be gathered from almost any poultry book, is well enough, we admit, and quite worthy of attention; but our objection to malt—putting aside its cost as a dietary article for chicken-feeding—is that it engenders "scouring" if continued for any length of time; but we have found from experiment that profitable results can be produced far more economically, and quite as expeditiously, by the use of

"Spratt's Granulated Meat Crissel," if judiciously employed.

Having now treated upon the system that should be carried out in stocking the poultry-yard, we must not forget that the female sex is thus far alone represented; and it is almost unnecessary to add that in choosing hens and pullets for this purpose that their plumage—which in this instance is really of secondary importance—should correspond with that of the cock bird in the main points of the breed, but that size and shape, which is of more consequence, should also be considered; and apart from any " fancy " pretentions, they should be healthy, full-grown, bright-looking, vivacious birds, and none of them less than a year old when bred from.

In the selection of a cock bird, his shape and size, gestures and movements, are alike important to the production of strong and healthy chickens. Liveliness and activity should characterise his every movement. He should have strong legs, supporting a broad body; he should carry himself with an air of self-importance and defiance, his eyes should be bright and restless, his comb and wattles of a brilliant red, and his plumage tolerably smooth and close. If he answers to this description, looks well, and pays proper attention to his consorts, such a bird as this cannot be too highly valued.

At two years of age we consider a cock to be in his prime, and if then mated with hens in their *second* season, we have always found a greater amount of stamina perceptible in the chickens than in those instances where the latter have been produced from younger parents. The vigorous nature, however, of the Houdan is not, we verily believe, to be surpassed by male birds of any other breed,—the game perhaps excepted —either for the early period it shows itself, or for the extent of its duration; and although very marked exceptions will occasionally arise in the instance of highly-bred specimens, they merely tend to make the fact more significant. In some of the French districts, where this race is *extensively cultivated*, it is nothing uncommon for a Houdan cock to be seen running with twelve, fifteen, and even a larger number of hens, and we have been assured that every egg laid as a rule proves prolific. Climate possibly influences this in no inconsiderable degree, but that it is not mainly dependent on such conditions we will put a crucial case in point :—

Not many months back an acquaintance, for experiment sake, let a three-year-old cock serve ten hens; seven-eights of the eggs were not only fertile, but resulted in the production of chickens with constitutions such as the most aspiring amateur would not fail to covet, for their iron-like tendency.

Respecting the precociousness of the cockerels, at little more than eight weeks old, we have found it frequently necessary to separate the sexes, the little rascals at this early age showing their naturally vigorous disposition. We have one cockerel hatched in March last, being, at the time we are writing, not yet two months old, who will answer the crow of his paternal relative in a manner as defiant as it is ludicrous; and, as showing the self-reliant and fearless disposition of the male chickens sometimes at a very early period, we will instance the following, which has reference to the cockerel in question :—A short time since we turned into the chicken run a Brahma hen, whose broody propensities we wished to check. Throwing down soon after a handful of barley to the chickens, she once or twice drove them off, and was appropriating to herself a much larger share than she was fairly entitled to, when our little hero, seeing the rapidity with which the grain was diminishing, to his and the other chickens' discomforture, "threw up" his feathers, and, to our surprise, flew at her in the most "game" manner possible, and although the contest appeared about as unequal as a giant and a pigmy doing battle (for she was a large hen and the cockerel was small for his age), he nevertheless completely beat her off, clapped his wings, and gave vent to a shrill but very exulting crow, as much as to say "try it again, if you dare, old lady." She gave him a wide berth after.

As it may possibly be inferred from this, that the cock birds evince a pugnacious disposition in some degree, to show this is very far from being the case, and as a remarkable instance of the uses that may be made of them in unusual capacities, the following is perhaps worth narrating :—Mrs. H—, an old and esteemed friend, had the misfortune for a Brahma hen to die suddenly, which had only the fortnight previously brought off a fine brood of nine Houdan chicks. Being rather early in the season, another hen to act as foster-mother could not at the time be obtained. Mrs. H— had no faith in "artificial" mothers, and was in danger of losing the brood, which was a valuable one. Narrating to us the awkward strait in which she was placed, whilst strolling round the yard, we remarked, in a small run, a Houdan cock intended for sale. The circumstance of cock Turkeys being somewhat extensively employed in certain parts of France for bringing up chickens, had never very favourably impressed us, as to its general adaptability in this country, until that moment; but we thought the opportunity a very eligible one for personally testing what capabilities a male bird really *did* possess for such an undertaking. At our suggestion the chicks were given to the cock in question—not without misgiving on the part of Mrs. H—. But her fears were of short duration, the " gentleman " looked at the little things for a minute or so, as if not quite satisfied with their intrusion, then called to them as he would to his hens, to which the chickens immediately responded. No hen mother could have been more careful, or more kind and attentive, than he proved himself to be, and it was really amusing when we saw him, about a week after, strutting about the yard—scratching for the little creatures, as seemingly pleased and proud of his charges as if he had hatched them. If, some months after, at the B—— Poultry Show, spectators of a pen of remarkably fine birds in the French class, to which the second prize was awarded, could have really known how the early days of the occupants of the pen in question had been passed, it would doubtless have attracted still greater attention.

Since then we have not failed to take a lesson from the incident we have recorded, for we have on sundry occasions let our old cock birds have the charge of chickens; and from the very satisfactory manner in which they have discharged their trust, we can unhesitatingly recommend the services of a feathered "step" father as being quite as economical and effectual, and at times far less troublesome, than that of an "artificial" mother.

But returning again to the practical management of the stock, the subject of drink and food merit special attention. As dirty or impure water materially detracts from the well-doing of poultry by germinating the seeds of disease, the importance of a continuous supply, pure and clean, cannot be too strictly insisted on. Any receptacle almost can be used for the purpose; but as we have ourselves derived so much satisfaction from the use of the water fountains, seen in Figs. 3 and 4, we have no hesitation in recommending their general adoption; one is of metal, the other earthenware, but both possessing decided advantages in point of ornament, usefulness, and economy, being cleaned in a moment, and not liable to get out of order.*

Respecting feeding, a somewhat different system must be

---

* For these, and for the majority of the illustrations of poultry appliances throughout this little work, we are indebted to Mr. F. Crook, the inventor and manufacturer, of 20, Motcombe Street, Belgrave Square, S.W.

substituted in confinement than where the fowls are running comparatively at large. The morning feed for our *adult*

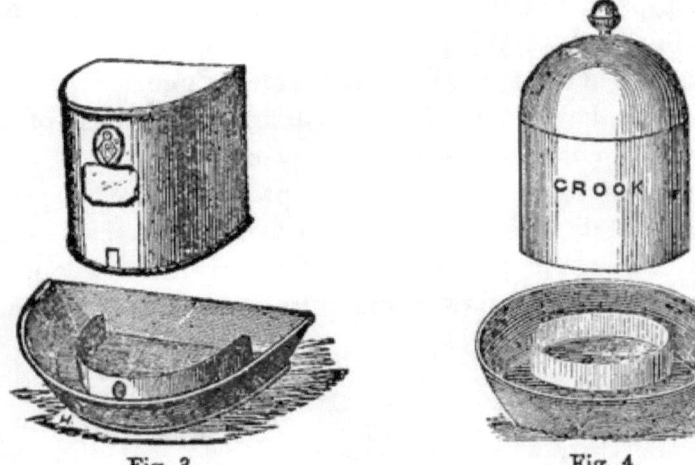

Fig. 3. Fig. 4.

stock has for some time past usually been equal parts of either barley-meal and toppings, varied by "Spratt's Poultry Food," or oatmeal, toppings, and boiled mashed potatoes, or even parings, with the "Granulated Meat Crissel" every

Fig. 5.

other morning, in the proportion of about a quarter of a pint to a dozen fowls, the whole mixed with water to such a consistency as to form a doughy paste, which, on being rolled out, can be divided into *patons* just large enough for the fowls to swallow with ease, and so that all have their fair proportion. In winter we mix the food with *boiling* water just sufficient to make the former "crumbly," frequently seasoning it with pepper, and always making it a point of giving it to the fowls while warm. When we formerly adopted the latter plan, we made use of a large shallow earthenware pan, for the ground being, as we have said, of loose earth, a receptacle of some kind was absolutely necessary to prevent waste. But, as it is the nature of fowls to scratch, this proved very inadequate to the purpose it was intended; the fact being that in their hungry endeavours to get it, the food was thrown about in all directions, trampled over, and quite as much spoilt as eaten; so we at last devised a roughly-framed cover with wire partitions to obviate this, and which was successful to a certain extent; but Mr. Crook has long since introduced two feeding appliances, Figs. 5 and 6, which carry out the purpose far more effec-

Fig. 6.

tually. The first, Fig. 5, is constructed for a dozen full-grown fowls to feed peaceably at one time, and Fig. 6 is not only a receptacle for food, but for water also if required. Being made of wrought iron and galvanized, they are both almost indestructible, and, from the facilities afforded for cleansing, are, in a sanitary sense, particularly serviceable.

Indian corn, both as meal and in grain, we once used largely; but from its too fattening tendency, which we shall always have cause to remember, we have quite eschewed it as being unsuitable diet for Houdans, unless they have an unlimited run, and even then we think they are better without it. Beyond an unlimited supply of green food, either grass, lettuce, or a fresh-pulled cabbage suspended by a string from the roof of the run for them to peck at, and plenty of clean water to drink, our *adult* stock, if confined, rarely ever have more than we have already enumerated until the evening, when a sufficiency of good heavy barley forms their concluding meal.

Fowls cannot be expected to lay freely if half starved, we admit; but, on the other hand, giving them too much food at one time, or giving it too often, is almost as great—indeed, we may say a far greater, evil; and, apart from serious consequences as those to which we will presently allude, an undue amount of food materially *decreases* not only the number, but even the size, of the eggs. In our opinion, the majority of adult fowls would be more profitable and better in condition if they were *under* rather than over-fed. The rule should be, never to satisfy their appetites to their fullest extent, for they, like children, will eat, if the opportunity but offers, considerably more than is beneficial to them. The above maxim should be strictly enforced where Houdans are concerned, particularly in confinement. The rapidity with which they, in common with most of the French breeds, naturally put on flesh and fat, make them invaluable as table-fowl; but where other objects are desired, such as good layers or the production of strong and healthy offspring, overfeeding should be carefully guarded against. The other extreme must not, of course, be pursued, or an empty egg-basket will be the result; but *sparse diet* should be the rule after chickenhood has passed, or untimely deaths in the poultry yard will spoil alike the pleasure and the profit. We have paid bitterly for our want of experience of this in our earlier acquaintance with the breed.

At the time we speak of we recollect how, with perhaps a

pardonable degree of pride, we inspected our stock the last thing at night, and congratulated ourselves upon the nice "plump" condition the birds were in. But our feelings may be imagined when, early one morning, we found a valuable hen dead upon the nest, and could not then assign a reason for the fact. We lost another, and yet another, in the same manner; the loss was getting serious, and we half made up our minds to have nothing more to do with the breed in question; we attributed this calamitous state of things, of course, to everything but the right cause. The following week we were almost at our wits' end by the further loss of three more fine, plump, and valuable hens, two in the above-named manner and the third by her suddenly falling lifeless at our feet. But the secret was now discovered. "Apoplexy, by Jove," said a friend emphatically, who was present at the time—and to whom we had been relating our grievances—"You've been giving them too much grub, and I shouldn't wonder, after what you've told me, that that accounts for the others going off so suddenly." Yes, *overfeeding* had done it all. We had "killed them with kindness." From that time we were more guarded in our system of feeding. We recruited our stock, put all our fowls on "shorter commons," and only fed them twice a day—morning and evening—with a limited allowance of food, which system we still adopt, and we have never since met with catastrophies of a similar kind.

But respecting "systematic" feeding, the ideas enunciated by Mr. Wright have hitherto more strictly accorded with our own in this particular.* "No fowls," he remarks, "require, at most, more than three meals per day, and, as a rule, do far better with two. The first should, or in confinement must, consist of soft or pulpy food of some kind, and be given early

---

* "Illustrated Book of Poultry," page 25.

in the morning. If the fowls be at liberty, or have grass runs, they should have nothing further until half an hour before they go to roost, when they should have a feed of grain. In point of quantity no fixed scale can be given; some breeds eat double the quantity of others, and even the same hen will require a very different allowance, according as she is laying or not at the time. Nevertheless, there is a rule, simply and easily understood, which will unfailingly secure both health and eggs, and that is to give the birds just as much as they will eat with an eager or ravenous appetite, and no more. We are speaking now of adult fowls, and such must on no account ever be allowed to have as much as they will eat; directly they cease to run, if the food is thrown to them, or commence "picking it over," if given in a trough or saucer, it should be stopped or taken away. On no account must there be any left.

"While no absolute scale can be given for the reasons stated, it will generally be found that hens of large breeds, when laying or moulting, require about as much meal or dough as will make a ball two and a half inches in diameter for their feed every morning, and a woman's handful—we mean with the palm downwards — of grain at night. Indeed, for large breeds, this "handful" system will generally be a safe one as regards the grain; but smaller fowls, from Spanish downwards, should have rather less, according to size. The only real rule, however, is that which we have given above, and we would add the caution that many on trial will not think it sufficient. We have often had visitors who have remarked that our fowls must be half starving, as they saw them fly up in the air when their breakfast was taken out to them. They are, in fact, always ready for food; but we are certain, from long experience, that this system of feeding is the best, not only for profit, but for really healthy condition.

"In bad or cold weather, or when moulting, a little more may be allowed; but we never allow our own birds—we speak of adults only—to eat to repletion. Such a course will always destroy the profit of poultry-keeping; at least, in a confined space. Even in strict confinement, where every atom of food must be supplied, there should not be a third regular meal, but simply a small handful of grain among every two or three birds, in proportion to their size, to afford them gratification and keep the appetite alive. Occasionally, in such circumstances, the diet may be varied by giving the handful each of grain in the middle of the day; and then, instead of corn, a very scanty feed of soft food, not more than half the breakfast, the last thing at night."

Although Houdans are designated as non-setters, after laying for many months in succession, as they will do, it is not at all uncommon for the hens occasionally to show a broody tendency; in the case of valuable birds, we never discourage it, but let them remain on the nest if so disposed for three weeks or a month, feeding them liberally, but still in moderation; by this rest we find their moult is considerably facilitated, and they begin to lay again much sooner than they would do otherwise, thus ensuring a good supply of eggs for early setting.

The hens of this breed are very seldom to be trusted for incubating their own eggs; therefore, one or two Brahma or other cross-bed fowls must be kept when chickens are wanted; but to impute to them the character of *never* sitting or hatching out a brood under "natural" conditions, is open to grave doubt, and in support of our assertion we have appended the notes of an esteemed correspondent, Mr. H. T. Dudgeon, of Ashford, Staines:—

"There is one remark made about certain breeds, viz., that they are everlasting layers, meaning, of course, birds that *don't* sit. The leading books and journals of the day will tell you a Spanish hen, a Hamburgh, or a Houdan will not sit, except she be 'one of those very rare exceptions to the almost invariable rule.' I totally deny this, though I know I take up a position at variance with every writer and breeder that I know of. I say every domestic bird will sit, and I would undertake to make them do so, whatever breed was brought me. There is no secret in it. Indeed I am surprised that such assertions should be made by so many practical people. I have found by trial, founded on theory, that all breeds sit. In this way, take a few of the so-called non-sitting breeds, give them unlimited range, particularly where there are coverts to lay away in; do not interfere with them at all; let them lay their eggs where they like; and, if moderately fed, they will lay in the spring. As soon as eleven or thirteen eggs are laid, *if never touched* or in any way disturbed, they will not fail to not only sit, but bring off and *rear* a healthy brood of chickens, be they Houdans, Hamburghs, Polands, Spanish, Crêves, La Flêche, Breda, Guinea Fowl, or what not. I was always of this opinion, contrary to that of all books or poultry periodicals I have seen, so determined to try it. What first made me think so was, that I noticed most of these "non-sitters," as soon as they began to moult about June or July, get a peculiar faint cluck when they were driven about, or whenever they ran quickly, spontaneously. This is not so apparent with birds of these breeds *unless* they have an unlimited range. My birds were left to find their own roost in the trees; and this fact, combined with an *unlimited* range—though it alters their time of moulting and duration of laying—never fails to rouse their dormant desire for the execution of the laws of nature. The only thing to be guarded against is having *too many* hens in trying this experiment, if any one should so desire, as there is a danger of their finding out another's laying nest, and so worry her out of it, and instead of a brood of chickens a lot of addled eggs would result."

Notwithstanding the high repute, both as layers and table-fowl in which Houdans are held, these qualities are capable of being yet *further improved* by a little judgment and patience. In considering, in the first place, how the egg-producing instinct may be enlarged, it is to be regretted that this trait has to a considerable extent been latterly neglected for points of a fancy nature entirely, and that competitors for prizes, to get their pullets into a suitable condition for showing, still *systematically* retard laying by every means in their power.

To these causes the deterioration of other breeds besides the Houdan, in an economical sense, may fairly be attributed. From the same causes may be traced the fact that good egg-producing fowls are, as a rule, not so plentiful as formerly. The point, therefore, to which we should direct our readers' attention is simply this, that any one rearing poultry as a matter of business should carry out the same care in selection as the fancier. Their views may be different, but the result will be the same. The one seeks beauty of form, the other the egg-producing capabilities of his poultry; and by due care and attention in selecting his stock, he will decidedly obtain it. In our dairy farms we observe the same thing. The best milking-cows, or those who produce the greatest quantity of milk, are invariably the offspring of cows known for their great milk-bearing qualities; therefore we should advise all who desire to have a poultry yard on a large scale, and at the same time to make it a profitable pursuit, to select their stock from breeds well known as first-rate egg-producers.

We need scarcely say, then, that the eggs from the best laying hens should alone be chosen for sitting; of the pullets hatched from them, those only partaking of their mother's special qualities again selected, and the process repeated until the desired object is attained.

As a table-fowl, again, although some strains will bear favourable comparison even now with the Dorking, as to quality and quantity of meat, by carrying out a similar proceeding as the above in the selection of stock, but directed of course to a different end, will show the merits of the Houdan in its fullest perfection. The farmer,* above any class of the

---

* "Farm-yards are seldom stocked with profitable poultry; in them, too often, is the pernicious adherence to the system of breeding in and in, seen in its worst aspect; the result is *certain* degeneracy. Farmers look upon poultry as a trifling and unimportant item in the farm stock, only to be kept as layers of eggs during summer, and are quite satisfied if their chickens bring a fair market price. But why not rear fowls that will weigh eight instead of four

poultry-breeding community, should achieve these results, for he has all the facilities for doing so advantageously, to the envy of many an owner of but a few yards of run. He has only to profit by the valuable precedent the French breeders have already established by mating *his* breeding stock in the same manner they have done generation by generation, and to the exclusion of all other points excepting those which are most admired in a table fowl, viz., short-legged, white-skinned birds, carrying an abundancy of flesh of good quality where the carver and his guests most appreciate it—the breast. The Houdan's economic worth in these particulars, notwithstanding what has already been accomplished in this direction, appears to us to have as yet far from attained its maximum, and we feel justified in giving it as our opinion, both from experiments we have made and witnessed, that the breed can be cultivated to surpass the Dorking in all those points for which the latter is most esteemed; but it must be done systematically, and bred *exclusively* for the points already mentioned, precisely the same as the Dorking itself has been brought to its present state of perfection as a table or market fowl, for it is material to bear in mind that no characteristics, whether viewed from fancy or economic principles, can be established unless it is *by breeding for them.*

---

pounds? and at the same cost of feeding. Surely such weights will command higher prices than merely those of the market, which is often supplied with birds scarcely worth the name of fowls, creatures of overy conceivable form and colour, with long black legs, narrow breasts, and twisted breast-bones, certainly possessing a superabundance of tail; but that adornment goes for little or nothing in the cook's eye. These miserable results are by no means the consequences of want of food. A farm yard is the paradise of poultry, and nowhere can they live in greater plenty or comfort. It is just because the birds want frame on which to put flesh and fat; bone is deficient, and all the lapsful of oats, barley, and wheat which the farmer's wife may filch for them from the gude man's barn are wasted on a worthless crew."—'The Hen-Wife,' *by the Hon. Mrs. Arbuthnot.*

The deep compact body of the Houdan, its broad breast, light pinky legs, and the small amount of bone and offal it has, compared to most fowls, is undeniable; and it has long been a matter of surprise why the breed has not been more largely cultivated in this country, as it combines the qualities most looked for and desirable in spring chickens, rapid growth being not one of the least of them. There appears to be less difficulty, too, in rearing Houdans than almost any other variety. There are fowls in plenty, we aver, that when *fully grown* are the *beau ideal* of hardihood, but very delicate *while* growing. But Houdan chickens, from the very day they are hatched, are strong and lively, and feather so very fast that they easily triumph over obstacles which would be death to any other breed; for the race seems to thrive almost as well on cold damp soils, with scarcely any care or attention, as they do in more favoured quarters, and when their wants and comforts are anticipated. Early chickens certainly pay the best; miserable skinny creatures will not, of course, command a remunerative price; but if they are really good-sized, plump birds, such as the cockerels especially will become on good feeding from twelve to sixteen weeks old, the demand is always more than equal to the supply; but meaty fowls can scarcely be expected from any breed without proper attention is paid to feeding; and to ensure fine chickens they should be fed from break of day, irrespective of the time of year. Barley-meal, oatmeal, and toppings, mixed warm, will bring them on wonderfully; and, if circumstances will admit of milk being given to them to drink, they will repay it by making flesh the faster, and by being ready for the market at an earlier date, will thus realize better prices.

The suitability of Houdans for early spring chickens certainly merits attention, and we cannot but endorse the testimony of writers who have preceded us respecting the very early period at which they are ready for the table, and what plump, fleshy, and toothsome fowls they really are; and the fifth toe—which although in our idea is certainly the only objectionable feature of the breed—is nevertheless no bad criterion of the fowl's value in the general estimation of the poulterers. We fully believe that, under favourable circumstances, no other breed can possibly compare with this, in the rapid manner with which they put on flesh as "chicklings." As an instance of this, last summer, whilst paying a professional visit to an agricultural acquaintance, and strolling over his farm, we were particularly impressed by the sight of some Houdans, which we knew were hatched the early part of the preceding March from our own eggs, being then, as nearly as possible, *thirteen weeks old.* "Ah!" said the farmer, noticing our look of evident pleasure, "I call those 'summut' like chickens." "They are the best sort I ever see." Come now, he continued, with a certain amount of pride, "I'll wager that the littlest of 'em weighs over three pun! and I'll bet you what yer like about it." "Perhaps you have weighed them already" was our rejoinder, smiling. "Oh, no I havn't," was the answer. But upon our declining, at all events, to stake anything on the doubt, yet being at the same time still very curious to ascertain what they really did weigh, a few of them were caught and placed in the scale; two of them (pullets) weighed respectively nearly three and a quarter pounds; another, three pounds and a half; and the joint weight of two cockerels turned the scale at seven pounds and three quarters. "How do you feed them, farmer?" we asked. "Oh, I give 'em warm soft mash in the morning early, and a good blow out of grain afore they go to roost; but atwixt you and me, Doctor, I don't believe so much in the grain, though I don't spare it either, but my opinion is, it's the precious lot o' slugs and worms they picks up as makes 'em so fat."

We perfectly coincided with the latter remark of our worthy old friend, for it instantly recalled to our recollection a very ingenious and economical method of feeding poultry for the market, which we witnessed some years ago whilst footing it through France; and as it may possibly afford some useful suggestions for large cultivators, it may perhaps be here worth recording:—

It was in the ploughing season, and by the wayside we noticed a large but rickety old caravan, somewhat similar to those used by our gipsies. Peeping in as we passed, we noticed that it was fitted up for fowls. It appeared that at that season an enterprising peasant bought a number of half-fed fowls at a low rate, hired the caravan, and took it to the field side. At break of day they were all let out to swarm over the fields, and gorge themselves with the worms which the ploughman turned up as he opened the furrows. The farmer was only too glad to get rid of the worms and slugs, and the poultryman to have his birds thus fattened. At sundown the birds were recalled by the enticement of a little barley or buckwheat, and were thus trained to come and roost in the caravan. During the day a young woman sat there in the shade, with her knitting needles, to mind the fowls, and the peasant, when he had done his day's work elsewhere, came back in the evening to examine them and to see that all was going on right, and, if necessary, to arrange for the shifting of quarters for the following day. By the time the ploughing of the district was finished, the fowls had attained a fair degree of fatness, and realised a good profit to their owner in the neighbouring market.

For the farmer, then, or to those who have space at their command, and are thus inclined to turn their attention to to poultry rearing for the market, thus adding an additional profit—and no inconsiderable one either—to their existing resources, the Houdan, it will be seen, offers unexceptionable opportunities.

Mr. Kinard Edwards, in a lecture delivered by him to the members of the Breconshire Chamber of Agriculture, entitled "The Poultry-yard and the Profits derived from it," in advocating a more extensive culture of poultry by our farming community, points out the following facts:—

"The cost of rearing a chick from the time it leaves the shell until it attains a marketable age—say fourteen to sixteen weeks—does not exceed 15d. to the farmer, as it must be remembered that he obtains their necessary food at wholesale prices. Well, at the age of sixteen weeks, you have a fowl or chicken weighing over 5½lbs., or 11lbs. the couple; such chickens will realize over 8s. at 9d. per lb. There can be no difficulty in getting such a price, for you can yourself see the market quoted weekly, and that fine, well-fatted chickens command 1s. per lb. in most of our large towns, and that poulterers are always ready to give an extra 2d. per lb. for a large, well-fatted chicken in preference to smaller birds. It is, however, necessary in keeping fowls for the production of meat, to keep a sufficient number, as the trouble is much the same to rear and send six or eight dozen to market as to send one dozen, and a smaller number will not pay for the necessary trouble and attention.

"The cost of rearing a chick to the average laying age, say seven months, does not exceed 1s 6d.; she then commences to return a profit for her food, and during the following two years will produce—Hamburghs, 440; Houdans, Leghorns, and Andalusians, 400 eggs per bird (from some of our previous remarks, it will have been gathered that we place a far higher standard on really *good laying strains* of Houdans than Mr. Edwards does). During these two years each bird will cost you, on an average, 1d. per head per week, allowing them to be well fed. Fowls that have a good grass run, as most farmers fowls have, can be kept in first-class condition at this cost, for it must be remembered that fowls gather a considerable quantity of food for themselves at no cost to their owner; they consume quantities of green food, such as grass, also seeds, waste grain, kernels, worms, slugs, grubs, flies, &c. Such feeding, added to the 1lb. or 18oz. of grain per week, will be found ample for the largest fowls. I purchase nearly all the grain I give to my fowls at retail prices, and I find that my fowls cost me less than 1d per week per head. Now let us come to the debtor and creditor account: cost of rearing chick to egg-producing age, 1s 6d.; two years' feeding at 1d. per week, 8s. 8d.; total cost, 10s. 2d. To set on the credit side, we have, say

440 eggs at 9d. per dozen, £1 7s. 6d.; the value of the hen killed at this age, at the rate of 4d. per lb., 2s 6d.; total £1 10s.; add to this the value of its manure during the two-and-a-half years—and on the value of fowl dung I shall have more to say further on—allowing 1oz. per day of dry dung to each fowl, will give 3s. 4d. at five shillings per cwt. This, added to the £1 10s., brings the total to £1 13s 4d. as the return from each fowl killed at the age of two-and-a-half years; deduct expenses or costs incurred, 10s. 2d., and we have a net profit from each bird of £1 3s. 2d., or over 200 per cent."

In thus giving a portion of Mr. Edwards' remarks, we must make due allowance for losses, deaths, &c., which he has apparently failed to take into consideration; and, on the whole, we should be inclined to look upon the sum set down for expenses as being insufficient. But after this is said, and full provision made for the above items, we think that Mr. Edwards has conclusively proved that poultry farming can be made sufficiently profitable to induce its more general adoption.

In reference to the value of the Houdan, as a cross with other breeds, we may as well say at once that, although some very valuable results may be obtained, such as a gain of *vigour* and *early maturity* such a cross possesses, so far as our actual experience has enabled us to ascertain, no merits whatever in *mere beauty of appearance,* but, on the contrary, certainly deteriorates it. In instances where hens of certain breeds have been employed as a cross with the Houdan cock, the undermentioned results have been noticed.

With the Spanish hen the production was a fowl of rather a nondescript character, so far as the plumage only was concerned, but an enormous producer of very large eggs, an excellent sitter, but rather an indifferent mother.

With the Cochin hen we get a bird also of common appearance, but the flesh is of good quality, although rather deficient in breast meat; it matures rapidly, and is an excellent sitter and mother. These fowls as chickens are rare specimens of hardihood, and feather infinitely faster than Cochins.

With the Brahma hen we have a fowl of rather small proportions as compared to some other crosses; but it matures early, the quality of the meat is not to be despised, and we get an astonishingly good layer and large eggs.

With the Dorking hen the plumage varies considerably—the chickens appear to almost always lay well—they are particularly hardy, and greatly surpass the Dorking breed itself in their early maturity and for the quantity and excellent quality of the meat. This is, perhaps, one of the very best crosses we are acquainted with. These chickens rapidly attain a great weight, and, when plucked, their fine white and fleshy bodies, and five toes, present a superior appearance.

High-class or prize stock may, if the farmer be at all ambitious of winning exhibitional honours, be also both economically and successfully raised under such unexceptional opportunities as a farm affords, and we should suggest the practicability in this case of his employing moveable houses without bottoms, for the fowls will thus give to the ground, in the shape of ordure, a far greater equivalent than the green food they rob it of. Such houses should be stationed so far apart that the mixture of the different broods is wholly prevented, and all the advantages of a wide range are obtained. Regarding the hens under this more natural condition of poultry-rearing during the hatching season, they should be provided with single coops, roofed and closed on all sides but the bottom and front. The form of one very generally known is represented by Fig. 7; but if further protected by what has been termed a "shelter board" in front, as suggested in "The Fanciers' Gazette," and which is easily affixed by a pair of hinges to the under side of the roof—thus being left open or closed as may be desired by a holdfast and staple—its utility will be greatly increased. These coops should be placed in any advantageous spot, either beneath the trees or elsewhere. This is the nearest affinity to game-rearing we are acquainted with, and has the same result in giving to the fowls a similar beauty of plumage so remarkable among all game birds in their native state. Another great advantage from this system is, that the hens never become unhealthily fat, but yet yield a very fair scale weight.

Fig. 7.

Where a well-kept lawn or paddock happens to be within the amateur's resources, the lively bearing and ornamental appearance of the Houdan is then seen to advantage; and a prettier sight on a fine day than a few properly-matched first-class birds of this breed, with their variegated black and white plumage and handsome crests, contrasting as they do so pleasantly with the green velvety turf, any lover of poultry could scarcely wish for. Under such conditions a similar plan may be followed as we have already recommended for the rearing of fancy poultry on a farm—viz., the use of moveable houses—for the stock can thus be kept with every facility, and the chickens be bred with very little trouble and expense.

E

It may not here, perhaps, be out of place if we observe that during the moulting season the sexes should be separated;—firstly, because the service of the male bird at this time is of little, if any, value,—and by thus parting the sexes at a comparatively early period of the year the eggs will show a higher degree of fertility; secondly, that when fowls are kept for fancy purposes, the incipient feathers of the hens would be injured by attentions simply of a vexatious and fruitless nature; and, further, that at this period there appears to exist a certain morbid irritability somewhat peculiar to all crested fowl, but more particularly conspicuous in the Polish and French breeds, of picking away one another's crest feathers whilst they are but partially developed. This practice not unfrequently exists in both sexes, but the crest of the male bird seems to suffer the most. As this proceeding, so far as we have noticed, appears more generally confined to the period stated, we have concluded, from the manner in which the cock will remain perfectly still and allow the budding feathers to be thus abstracted by the hens, coupled with the sense of positive relief which it seems evidently to afford him, that irritation of a very excessive kind manifests itself at this period, and at this particular spot, and which is, perhaps, attributable to the length of time these feathers will sometimes remain in the sheath. Under these circumstances, nature seems to have endowed the crested fowls with the instinct of mutual assistance. They work upon the old motto, "Scratch me, and I'll scratch you;" but in their great desire to aid and relieve each other, often produce a disfigurement grievous to the eye of their owner.

Closely allied to this proceeding is another which is occasionally productive of annoyance in confined yards,—it being that Houdans,* not content with plucking out the crest feathers as

---

* We were some years back disposed to believe that this habit was special to the breed in question; but we find, in course of correspondence, that it is not

already narrated, at times will take a fancy to other portions of one another's plumage, and actually devour it. The cause of this morbid appetite has hitherto remained unexplained, although various reasons have been assigned and remedies without number suggested. Uncleanliness, insufficiency, or even a superabundance of animal food, thirst, and want of occupation, have all been adduced on not at all unfounded grounds as being directly or indirectly the origin of it. In alluding to this unnatural habit, Mr. Wright, in his compendious poultry work, attributes *thirst* especially, as being *directly* accountable, and gives his grounds for such an inference, thus :—

"We have again and again seen it commence when the fountain was empty or absent, or filled with sun-warmed water, and have verified the conclusion repeatedly by withholding water from a hen known to be addicted to it for a few hours in warm weather. The inference is obvious; keep *cool* fresh water *always* in reach, and many cases at least would be avoided. *Idleness* is also a great cause, and we have known a whole yard cured by burying corn in the ground so as to give the birds occupation in scratching. It is for this very reason useful to hang up a whole cabbage by a string just within reach of the birds; by its bobbing about it gives occupation and green food at the same time. By combining such measures with the medical treatment given,* and secluding any particularly wicked fowl till the habit be in a measure forgotten,

---

so, and that amongst Malays, Brahmas, Cochins, and Polish, it has recently been very prevalent.

* One-fourth of a grain of acetate of morphia daily, and twice a week a grain of calomel; these, combined with carbonate of potass sufficient to give the water an alkaline taste, is the remedy alluded to by the writer, with the further external application of carbolic disinfecting soap made into a stiff lather, so as to render the parts where the tops of the feathers have been removed, less attractive to the fowls' palates.

and any bleeding one till healed, we believe this disgusting appetite may be successfully checked in the majority of cases."

It is worth remarking that we have had considerably fewer cases of this kind amongst our own fowls since "bone meal" has entered into our category of poultry-food, and which was inadvertently omitted when describing our own system of feeding, but concerning which a word or two will be found in another chapter.

We have found that during the last few years the cock birds, after their second season, have been rather susceptible to their feet becoming "corny." The affection (which in the Dorking is commonly known as "bumble-foot") manifests itself by a small corn or ulcer at the bottom of the foot; with time it increases in size, ulcerates in a more or less degree, lameness ensues, and, *if neglected*, the bird after a time becomes a useless appendage to the establishment. As no other class of large and heavy fowl that we are aware of, save the Dorking, appears to suffer from it, the high perches and the hard gravelled yards which have been so frequently ascribed as its *chief* cause does not, in our belief, afford a satisfactory solution; they may, we admit, accelerate the mischief, but are, we cannot convince ourselves, the exciting causes of it. We adhere to the opinions of others, already promulgated, that to the extra toe—which ought not in any large breed to have been perpetuated—the real cause must be looked for. It is a startling fact that the complaint never made its unwelcome appearance in the Houdan until the fifth toe became an established requirement; for, even now, so far as we have been enabled to ascertain from various sources, it rarely, if ever, appears in the four-toed birds.

If the mischief has been allowed to proceed to any great extent unnoticed, or uncared for, it is almost a fallacy to attempt doctoring "from the low state of vitality," as remarked by Mr. Tegetmier, "existing in the feet of birds, and the inability to rest them when diseased;" but in early stages we have successfully adopted a somewhat similar course of treatment* as that also recommended by Mr. Wright. A low platform, littered with straw, is the best roost the bird can have until it has entirely recovered; indeed, we object at any time to high perches; to broad and flattish ones, and very low, we now give our decided preference.

The chief objection made by unappreciative neighbours to the keeping of fowls in town yards or gardens is the vocal serenade they are favoured with at day-break by the "lord of the harem." It is only a natural effort, of course, for him thus to exercise his throat and lungs; but, in confinement, he really seems to persevere with even still greater vehemence, simply we suspect, like Molly Bawn's lover, "because he's nothing else to do." Happily, however, the crow of the Houdan will bear favourable comparison—that is to say, if there be any question of tastes—with the hoarse volubility of the Cochin, or the very loud and prolonged solo of the Brahma; neither is it as shrill as in many other breeds.

As staunch supporters of the Houdan we have at times, when advocating its manifold excellences, been met with the remark—by ladies particularly—that nothing would induce

---

* "Some cases appear incurable, but if taken in good time, the daily application of lunar caustic, in the ordinary manner, will often effect a cure or the pigment of iodine of the British Pharmacopœia may be daily painted over the spot with a brush. Later on actual excision becomes necessary. In cases where the tumour is soft and full of pus, or in the form of an abscess, a free puncture may be made, after which the matter is pressed out, the part fomented with warm water, and, after a day or two, caustic applied as already directed. In other cases the tumour appears hard, and the incision should be made in the form of a cross, when a sharp squeeze will generally expel the offending matter through the wound."—"The Illustrated Book of Poultry," page 186.

them to keep top-knotted fowls of any kind, for the simple reason that they have heard that crested birds are always more or less infested with parasites. From careful observation we cannot refrain from believing that if ever such a state of things has been found to exist, it has proceeded, not from any peculiar predisposition in the breed itself, but from culpable neglect or want of attention to their commonest requirements, the same as in all fowls. For where they have the opportunity of revelling at will in their heap of sand or dry sifted road-side grit—which is as important to them as the bath is to man—no fowls will be cleaner in this respect.

We maintain that if cleanliness is properly observed, Houdans, no more and no less than the rest of their feathered kind, should enjoy perfect immunity from tormenting strangers of an insect description. If poultry-keepers would only follow our own example by never admitting a purchased bird without previous careful examination, and if, upon there being the slightest indication of such uncleanliness as we speak of, make liberal use of a common pepper-castor containing carbolic powder, Persian powder, or even ordinary powdered sulphur, and dust the contents once or twice, or oftener if necessary, well into the roots of the feathers, and keep the fowl where it can have a dust bath to itself, there would be, we are convinced, little cause for such complaints as these.

CHAPTER III.

FATTENING — THE ENGLISH AND FRENCH SYSTEMS DESCRIBED — ITS RELATIVE VALUE IN A DOMESTIC AND COMMERCIAL SENSE.

THE rapid flesh-acquiring properties of the Houdan, as befitting it for the spit iu an incredibly short period, we have already shown in the preceding chapters; but this natural predisposition to make flesh has given a stimulus to the art by which the process is increased, and both weight and appearance still further improved, and this seems a fitting opportunity for making a few observations respecting it.

It is no use denying the fact that fowls are bought to please the eye by their whiteness and extraordinary size, far more than to gratify the palate. A well-fed chicken, however plump and tender, could not compete in the market with one which has been skilfully fattened. The latter would realize more money, even though the fat which had been forced upon it either found its way into the dripping-pan or marred the delicate flavour of the flesh.

We hold that it is quite unnecessary to cram or otherwise force the fattening of the better breeds of fowls, and the cross breeds from them—as unnecessary as it is to whip and spur a horse that is eager to put forth his full power. If we kill a fowl for our own eating, or to share with a friend who can really appreciate what is put before him, we never put the knife into a fattened one. We should take up a young cockerel of three or four months old with an empty crop—a Houdan or La Flêche, or a cross betwecn either and a Dorking. From the time the bird was hatched—in our own estimation

—he has been prepared for the table by being properly fed and well cared for. He has known no irritating confinement, and has needed nothing but what he took eagerly as it was scattered at early dawn and dewy eve, or what he found in his rambles in the fields and hedge-rows. To cram such a fowl would be, in our opinion, wasteful as well as cruel. We say wasteful, as it really would be, when fowls are not reared for the market; but the fact, unfortunately, must be recognised that it is *not* wasteful when we look to the market value of the bird. So long as people will have fattened fowls, so long will the latter be the subjects of ingenious inventions to gratify the demand.

Further, the fattening process enables an old or inferior bird to "take the shine out of" a young one naturally fed, in the eyes of most purchasers. The dealers get a better price for them, and consequently they will be supplied. If we wish to keep fowls profitably for market purposes, it is then evident we must fatten them, and in order to do so as quickly and as economically as possible, we must do it systematically.

In former times, a few barn-door fowls were put into a coop with a railed bottom to allow the droppings to fall through. The fowls were regularly fed three or four times a day with barley-meal, giving them as much as they could be induced to eat at each meal, and no more. Some farmer's wife or daughter hit upon the improvement of keeping the birds in a state of darkness during the intervals between their meals, by having a cloth to drop at pleasure over the front. This made the fowls more ravenous when it was lifted. Of course the fowls were taken from the same run, so that there was no fear of any fighting, and the only struggle was how, in blissful ignorance, to achieve the object of their owner. If birds quarrel, it is, of course, useless to attempt fattening them together. Gradually it was found that fowls of each sex were better cooped together, even to the extent of being removed from the sound of each other's voices, which reminded them that they might have been hatched for something besides eating.

Another henwife, a cleanly woman, found that lime-whiting the hen-coop to prevent the annoyance of the birds by vermin and placing them in a snug warm corner, away from all draughts, increased the comfort of the fowls, and gave them, in short, nothing to do or to think about but eating and digestion, and thus enabled her to make a better show and suffer fewer disappointments on the subsequent market-day. The fowls were likewise kept scrupulously clean, and water, as much only as they would drink, was given with the food.

Regularity in feeding the fowls, when thus confined, was another improvement. Then came the food. Barley-meal alone gave place to a mixture of barley-meal and oatmeal. Sifted buckwheat meal was fancied by others, whilst all seemed to acknowledge that some of the skim milk which the pigs relished so much, made both barley-meal and oatmeal more nutritious and tasty than simple water for the fowls. Then the milk was warmed before mixing, and so, like all great inventions, the process of development was gradual. Many things, of course, were tried and pronounced failures. With these, however, we need not here concern ourselves.

When fattening was carried on, on an extensive scale, as in the neighbourhood of Dorking, for the London poultry market, the birds were, in a rough kind of way, crammed; but we question much whether they would not have done as well without that treatment. Sixteen or eighteen days was deemed a sufficient time to keep a fowl imprisoned before execution. If left any longer, he was liable to waste away, and if he did not fatten in that time, it was not economical to give him any more. It was found best to clear the whole lot off, fresh lime-white the coop, and begin again with another lot, for it would never do to clear out the fattened ones and supply their places with others. It was long ago an accepted maxim with henwives that fowls of different degrees of fatness should not be cooped together. The age at which the birds were cooped for fattening depended much upon the breed, or rather the growth of the bird. Generally, it was any time between three and six months, according to the demand. Frequently an old feather-eating or egg-eating hen has been put into the coop, as into a "Rachel bath," to recover the appearance of youth. We have known such a thing as a six-year-old hen, past laying, and apparently valueless, reappear from the coop to die, coupled with a plump young cockerel, and be selected by a purchaser in the open market. There is no doubt, then, that cooping and fattening improve the appearance of the fowls when trussed for the purchaser, and we may sum up the experience of the old farmers' wives who made a practice of it in a few words.

They put a lot of birds of the same sex, and from the same pen, together in a lime-whited coop, scrupulously clean, with a lathed floor. They shut them up in darkness, except when at regular intervals they fed them, in a warm snug corner free from draughts or other annoyances. They fed them on barley-meal and oatmeal, mixed with warm milk. They killed them at the end of sixteen or twenty days.

Thus much for the English practice. But the French, who created and gratified the taste for *pâtes de foies gras,* soon turned this rude practice into a fine art. They found in their own country the finest breed of fowls in the world for their flesh-acquiring qualities, and by the practice of their art they have certainly succeeded in rendering good birds extraordinary ones. The ordinary English coop, which, in an improved form, is still manufactured and extensively used here, and of which an illustration is given in Fig. 8, is in France contracted into a series of narrow compartments, eight inches wide, so that the fowls cannot turn round. The outer walls and partitions are closely boarded, the bottom only made with rounded spars of one and a half inches in diameter, running lengthways of the coop, on which the fowls perch, their dung falling between the bars. The top consists of a sliding door nearly as wide as the compartments by which the chickens are taken in and out. These fattening coops, constructed on either plan, we may observe, can now be obtained of Mr. F. Crook.

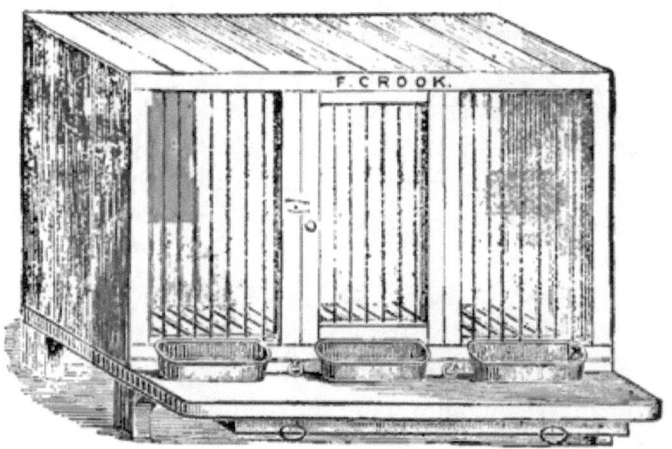

Fig. 8.

From the time the birds are put into these "condemned cells," until the moment they are taken out for execution, the only comfort they derive is the food which they receive, and this depends entirely upon the judgment of the feeders, for the food which, in English coops, the birds take eagerly, is in the French plan administered by the attendant. It is dough composed of buckwheat-meal and milk, cut up into rations and subdivided into "patons" about the size of a woman's finger. These boluses are soaked in water, put into the mouth of the bird, and rammed with the forefinger well into the gullet. This is continued until the attendant's notion of the bird's wants is satisfied. "It may happen that the tracheal artery is compressed with the gullet, which makes the creature cough, *but it is not of any serious consequence.*" The whole system is, however, minutely described in a translation of Mdlle. Millet Robinet's treatise, "Oiseaux de Basse-Cour," which appeared in the Royal Agricultural Society's Journal. The food, we are there told, is thus administered:—

"The attendant puts on an apron which will stand being soiled or torn, and takes the pullets on a board, with a bowl of clean water, then takes the first fowl from its cage, gently and carefully, not by the wings or the legs, but with both hands under the breast. She then seats herself with the fowl upon her knees, putting its rump under her left arm, by which she supports it. With the left hand the mouth is opened, which with a little practice becomes easy, and with the right hand takes up a pellet, soaks it well in the water (this is essential), shakes it on its way to the open mouth, puts it straight down, and carefully crams it with the forefinger well into the gullet. When it is so far settled down that the fowl cannot eject it, she presses it down gently with the thumb and forefinger into the crop, taking care not to fracture the pellet, for if some scraps of it remained in the gullet they might cause inflammation. Other pellets follow, until the feeding is complete. The fowl when fed is again held with both hands under its breast, and replaced in its coop without fluttering it. And so on with each fowl."

The utmost punctuality in feeding is insisted on to avoid loss of weight, either by keeping the stomach idle or by overloading it and causing indigestion. In this way, beginning with two or three pellets a meal, the number is daily increased until it reaches twelve to fifteen pellets. The crop is handled at each meal to see that the last is properly digested. If it is not, a meal is omitted. Two or three weeks, it is said, is time enough for ordinary fattening, but for extra fat poultry from twenty-five to thirty days are allowed. An average fowl takes, it is said, rather more than a peck of buckwheat to fatten it. Full directions are given for killing the unfortunate fattened prisoner, but they do not differ from the ordinary practice pursued by every one who keeps fowls for the table. The fowl has, of course, previously fasted for ten or twelve hours, and is then either stuck in the mouth deep enough for the knife to enter the brain, or a largish wound is made just below the ear. Immediately after the bird is stuck, it should be hung up to allow it to bleed freely, the head being held so as to prevent any violent fluttering. The free bleeding insures whiteness of the flesh.

The difference mentioned by Madlle. Millet-Robinet between 'fattened" and "extra-fattened" reminds us that in the French markets they have "half-fatted" and "fully-fatted" fowls. The fully-fattened ones will frequently realize as much as fifteen francs each, and, nevertheless, the half-fattened ones are preferable to them for eating. In the French markets these fully-fattened fowls present an appearance of having scarcely any bones. Their bodies look more like portions of legs of lamb than fowls. This peculiarity is produced by their being bandaged, when killed, to the desired shape; they are then wrapped in clean linen rags, which have been soaked in milk, so as to give an additional pearly whiteness to the skin. The Houdan and La Flêche birds are more especially treated in this way. In fact, these are the breeds which the French are most partial to, and of which the heavily-fattened fowls chiefly consist.

There is yet another experiment in the art of fattening fowls, which we owe likewise to our neighbours, and which has been used for many years in the best French poultry districts. It is by feeding the birds with semi-fluid meal. The fowls are caged as before described; but instead of the pellets, some meal without the husk is mixed with equal parts of milk and water till it assumes the form of thin gruel. This is poured down the bird's throat, by means of a funnel made of ordinary tinned iron, just large enough to contain one meal. The bird is held between the knees; with one hand the head is stretched out, the beak is opened, and the funnel is introduced with the other, right into the bird's throat. It requires a little tact to avoid injuring the throat, and, still further to prevent any mishap of this kind, the small end of the funnel is either furnished with a thin rim or covered with india-rubber. When the funnel is fairly introduced, it is filled by a ladle from a vessel placed beside the operator, who feels the crop to ascertain when it is full, and, if necessary, to hasten the passage of the food into it.

This rude way of administering the fluid food has been improved upon. A machine has been invented to *shoot* it into the bird's crop. A cylinder, with a neck at the end, shaped something like a champagne bottle, is filled with the food; the operator takes the bird in both hands, opens its mouth, inserts the nozzle, presses the treadle with his foot—this being connected with a piston inside the cylinder—and squirts the meal into the bird's crop. By this way, it is said, two hundred birds can be fed in an hour.

A similar plan of cramming the fowls has been invented in this country by Mr. F. Crook (see illustration, Fig. 9). Instead of the treadle, he uses a rack and pinion, and this necessitates two persons to work it instead of one; but the wants of a larger number of fowls can be provided for in a like period. When required for use the cylinder is brought into an upright position by means of a pivot. It is then filled with the liquid food and returned to its horizontal position. The flexible nozzle is inserted in the bird's throat, and the piston which ejects the food from the cylinder is moved by the rack and pinion. It will be seen by the illustration that the wheel has three handles. One-third of a turn injects a sufficient quantity into the fowl's crop. In the French system a graduated dial is fixed to the machine to regulate the quantity of food for fowls of different ages or of different degrees of fatness.

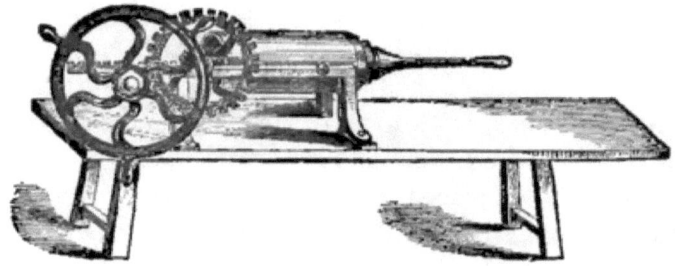

Fig. 9.

Such are the inventions which the rage for fat poultry has, it may be said, necessitated on the part of those breeders who supply the market. Nothing of the kind is really necessary for those who supply their own tables, and are anxious only to provide their guests with something worth eating rather than looking at. We are told by one inventor that the fowls seem to like the injecting process. We can understand their being glad when that and the three weeks' roost on a barred floor is over, and can believe that it makes death *quite a luxury to them.* It is a little to be preferred, perhaps, to starvation; but the two extremes meet very nearly, we fancy, on the score of cruelty, and every lover of poultry will rejoice when the disgusting fashion which demands such treatment passes away in favour of one more wholesome and natural.

An indirect mode of fattening fowls—and one which is extensively practised, not only in France, but in every country where the rearing of poultry is regarded as a business, and where it is carried out in the most thorough manner—is by destroying their reproductive organs, and turning the young cockerels into what are subsequently called *capons*, and the pullets into what are by the French called *poulardes*. It is an acknowledged principle—and the practice of it is a sign of civilization—that all animals thus deprived increase wonderfully in flesh, and likewise in the delicacy of it; and we can instance for size the " no sex " classes of our cat-shows. We may also refer to the oxen and sheep, which are in this respect the delight of our markets and our tables.

Caponising and poularde-making are not very extensively practised in England. We are not sufficiently advanced in the art of making a fine-looking dish; and really, when we consider that the poor fowls have to die for our delectation, we think, as there are plenty to supply us, it is hardly worth while to impose any further pain upon them. Without questioning the matter as to oxen and large animals, we do not believe that any man, blind-folded, could discover the particular delicacy of a capon or poularde above that of an ordinary pullet or cockerel. For our own eating, therefore, and for our own table, we hold it to be unnecessary.

It is said by some writers that the fowls feel no pain under the operation. We will believe it *when we have the fowl's evidence*, and not before. Nevertheless, having given our own opinion, we must admit that, commercially, fowls so treated have a higher value, and consequently, as long as the consumers ask for them and will have them, they must be supplied. This being the case, we have to consider how best to supply the demand with the greatest profit to the rearer. The better and more skilful the operation, the more satisfactory will it be to the owner, as the bird will the sooner recover, and commence to repay the owner by acquiring the desired size.

We have said that the English do not systematically practise the art. Our French friends do, and to them we must look for guidance in it. We have it best described in the work already referred to by Madlle. Millet-Robinet, quoted by Mr. Tegetmier.* She says:—

"The name of capon is given to young cocks which have been deprived of the faculty of reproduction. In this state they grow to a very large size, and fatten more readily; their flesh, also, is more delicate.

"It is desirable to submit the cocks to the operation when they are about four months old, and it is very important to choose a time when the weather is somewhat cool, rather moist than dry, and especially to avoid performing the operation during the great heats of summer.

"The instrument employed in the operation should be very sharp. A surgeon's small operating knife, termed a curved-pointed bistoury, is far better than an ordinary knife, as it makes a much neater wound and so increases greatly the chances of healing; or a curved-pointed penknife may be used. A stout needle and waxed thread are also requisite. A small curved surgical needle will be found much more convenient in use than a common straight one.

"It is necessary that there should be two persons to perform the operation. The assistant places the bird on its right side on the knees of the person who is about to operate, and who is seated in a chair of such a height as to make his thighs horizontal. The back of the bird is turned towards the operator, and the right leg and thigh held firmly along the body, the left being drawn back towards the tail, thus

---

* "The Poultry Book," page 139.

exposing the left flank where the incision has to be made. After removing the feathers, the skin is raised up, just behind the last rib, with the point of the needle, so as to avoid wounding the intestines, and an incision along the edge of the last rib is made into the cavity of the body sufficiently large to admit of the introduction of the finger. If any portion of the bowels escape from the wound, it must be carefully returned. The forefinger is then introduced into the cavity, and directed behind the intestines towards the back, somewhat to the left side of the middle line of the body.

"If the proper position is gained (which is somewhat difficult to an inexperienced operator, especially if the cock is of full size), the finger comes into contact with the left testicle, which, in a young bird of four months, is rather larger than a full-sized horse bean. It is moveable, and apt to slip under the finger, although adhering to the spine; when felt it is to be gently pulled away from its attachments with the finger, and removed through the wound—an operation which requires considerable practice and facility to perform properly, as the testicle sometimes slips from under the finger before it is got out, and, gliding amongst the intestines, cannot be found again readily; it may, however, remain in the body of the animal without much inconvenience, although it is better removed, as its presence is apt to excite inflammation.

"After removing the left testicle, the finger is again introduced, and the right one sought for and removed in a similar manner. It is readily discovered, as its situation is along-side of the former, a little to the right side of the body. Afterwards the lips of the wound are brought together, and kept in contact with two or three stitches with the waxed thread. No attempt should be made to sew up the wound with a continuous seam, but each stitch should be perfectly separate, and tied distinctly from the others.

"In making the stitches great care should be taken; the skin should be raised up so as to avoid wounding the intestines with the needle, or including even the slightest portion of them in the thread—an accident that would almost inevitably be followed by the death of the animal.

"After the operation the bird should not be permitted to roost on a perch, as the exertion of leaping up would unquestionably injure the wound. It should, therefore, at roosting time, be turned into a room where it is compelled to roost on the floor, previously covered with some clean straw. After that the bird had better be put under a coop in a quiet situation, and supplied with drink and soft food, such as sopped bread. It is best, after a few hours, to let him have his liberty, if he can be turned out in some quiet place removed from the poultry yard, as, if set upon by the other male birds, the healing of the wound would be endangered.

"For three or four days after the operation the bird should be fed on soft food. After that time it may be set at liberty for a short period, until it has recovered entirely from the operation, when it should be put up to fatten.

"In France it is customary to cut off the combs of the capons. This is regarded as a distinguishing mark of the operation having been performed, and consequently the birds do not sell so freely if they are allowed to remain.

"If the animal mopes about on the day following the operation, it is desirable to look at the wound, and, should it be inflamed, to bathe it with a little tepid water. If, however, the intestine has been wounded, there is no chance of recovering. Some persons place oil and other applications on the wound, but there is no doubt that they retard the healing process. As a rule, it may be stated that if the operation has been skilfully performed it rarely fails of success."

"It is a very singular fact," remarks Mr. Tegetmier, "that

after giving the above specific and very correct details of the operation of caponizing, the author of the treatise denies the possibility of making what are termed 'poulardes,' that is, pullets deprived of their power of reproduction in order to induce them to fatten rapidly, and states that the birds which are sold under that title are simply pullets fattened before they have commenced to lay.

"The operation is, however, much easier than the corresponding one on the cocks. The pullet is to be placed in the same position on the lap of the operator, the left leg being drawn forwards so as to expose the left flank, in which a longitudinal incision is to be made close to the side bone; this will bring to view the lower bowel, and along side of it will be found the egg-passage or egg-pipe. If this is drawn to the orifice of the wound by a small hooked wire, and cut across—or what is perhaps better, a very short piece of it removed—the development of the ovary, or egg-producing organ, is entirely prevented, and the birds fatten rapidly, attaining also a very large size. It is most important to perform the operation before the pullets have begun to lay.

"We would beg to impress most strongly the desirability of practising these operations, in the first instance, on dead birds of the same age, so that the operator may become acquainted with the situation and appearance of the parts concerned. By this means a greater amount of success will be obtained in the first instance, and much unnecessary suffering saved to the animals."

Respecting the value of capons for other purposes besides eating, on the Continent they are employed instead of hens for taking charge of young broods of chickens, and which these "no-sexed" birds—from their larger size and plentitude of feathering—it is asserted perform quite as efficiently; and if we may judge of this, from our own experience of our old cock birds in this capacity, and as mentioned in the preceding chapter, we see no reason to question it. The plan adopted abroad is described by Mr. W. M. Lewis, thus:—

"The moment the chickens are hatched they are taken from the hens and given to a capon, who rears them with all the care of a parent, often having a small bell attached to his neck, the tinkling of which serves the purpose of keeping the brood near him, similar to the clucking and maternal sounds of the mother. Should he show a disposition to treat the young chickens roughly at first, he may be confined alone for a day or two in a dark place, after which, if they be put with him, he will be pleased with their company and continue to take care of them. The hens are cooped and well fed until they regain the flesh and strength lost while sitting, and then turned out to lay again. In this way the poulterer is enabled to raise a large number of chickens from a few hens, and the capon generally brings double or treble the price of common poultry."

Like everything else, there is a right and wrong method in poultry-fattening, and as the preceding writer has observed, "a long and a short mode of accomplishing the object desired." For while on the one hand many classes of our poultry-breeding community who really profess to supply the market, yet leave their fowls to themselves, and in a great measure depend upon their ultimate marketable condition for the waifs and strays of sustenance which the birds are obliged to seek for themselves in the best way they can—another portion (and by far the most sensible) constantly supply their stock, as they would machines, with a proper sufficiency of suitable material, and which is thereby quickly converted into a nutritious article of diet. It therefore appears evident, —in spite of some of the disadvantages attached to high feeding where the egg-product only is required—that the best manner of fattening Houdans for the market, and where such is made a true business pursuit, to make it a profitable one also, *constant high keep from the very earliest days of chickenhood* is the rule to be pursued, as they are then always ready for the market with little or no preparation.

In concluding this portion of our subject, a few remarks which we take from "The People's Practical Book" on "picking and packing" the fowls may possibly prove of service to those who may be inclined to engage largely in the branch of commerce we have been discussing.

"The mode of picking while the bird is warm is called 'dry picking,' and is the favourite method of dressing poultry for the Philadelphia market. There is one objection to this system—that it does not improve the appearance, although it does the flavour; and while cooking, it will "plump up" and come out of the oven looking much finer than it went in. In addition, it will keep much longer than when dressed on any other plan. Another method is, after the bird is picked as above described, to plunge it in a kettle of very hot water, holding it there long enough to cause the bird to "plump," then hang it up by the foot until thoroughly cooled. This scalding makes the fat look bright and clear, and the fowl to appear much fatter than it would if picked dry."

"On the subject of boxing poultry for market, Dr. Bennet says—"It should be carefully packed in baskets or boxes, and, above all, it should be kept from the frost. A friend of mine, who was very nice in these matters, used to bring his birds to market in the finest order possible, and always obtained a ready sale and the highest market price. His method was to pluck them dry while warm, and dress them in the neatest manner; then to take a long, deep, narrow, tight box, with a stick running from end to end of the box, and hang the birds by the legs over the stick, which prevents bruising them or disfiguring them in the least." The way poultry is frequently forwarded to city markets is enough to disgust almost any one, and throws odium on breeders as a class.

"All poultry should be thoroughly cooled before packing. Then provide boxes; place a layer of rye straw that has been thoroughly cleansed from dust on the bottom. Commence packing by bending the head of the fowl under it; then lay it in the left-hand corner with the head against the end of the box, with the back up; continue to fill that row in the same manner until completed; then begin the second row the same way, letting the head of the bird pass up between the rumps of the two adjoining ones, which will make it complete and solid. In packing the last row reverse the order, placing the head against the end of the box, letting the feet pass under each other; should there be a space left between these two rows wide enough to lay in a few sideways, do so, passing the feet under the same way; but, should it not be wide enough, then fill up tight with straw, so that the poultry cannot move. This gives an uniformity of appearance and a firmness in packing that will prevent moving during transportation. Over this layer place straw enough to prevent one layer coming into contact with the other; then add other layers, packed in the same manner, until the box is filled.

"Care should be taken to have the box filled full, in order to prevent any disarrangement of the contents; for, should they become misplaced, the skin may become so badly disfigured as to cause a depreciation of the value to the owner. Great care should be taken, in packing, not to skin the bird, for during transportation the skinned places turn black and make it look badly. To those having extra fine poultry to send to market we should advise paper to be put over each layer before placing the straw on it; this prevents the dust settling on it, and adds much to its appearance.

"A little practice will soon make a person quite expert in packing, and an expert packer is valuable; his skill will pay the owner ten times his cost, for very frequently the first sight of a box of poultry sells it.

"To those wishing to market capons we would say they should be dry picked, with the feathers on around the head and the tip of the wings; also the tail feathers left in; the small, or pin feathers, should be all removed."

CHAPTER IV.

POULTRY-FANCYING, AND WHAT IT NECESSITATES.

SO far it will have been seen that we have directed our attention to the Houdan solely on its economic bearings. We now, however, enter upon the subject exclusively from a fancier's point of view; and, in doing so, it will scarcely be deemed inconsistent if we make a few general remarks ere we enter into details.

The fanciers of poultry may be divided into two very distinct classes, namely, amateurs, who take up the matter as a pursuit from which they are careless as to the question of gain; and "professional" fanciers, who are not without a dash of the amateur in their proceedings, but who keep an eye to the question of profit or loss in their attempts to improve the breed in which they take most interest, and take care that their yearly account of expenses and receipts, shows a balance in their favour. The well-known names in the catalogues corresponding to the pens, which, as the winter approaches, are filled with rare and beautiful birds at Birmingham, the Crystal Palace, and elsewhere, would, upon analysis, prove the truth of this classification.

The latter class is by far the larger of the two; and as plain figures are more convincing than mere general statements, we have no hesitation in citing the experience of a large breeder of "fancy poultry" in the Eastern counties, "that after the payment of his expenses, journeys to poultry shows, and interest of money expended on his premises, his clear profit from prizes, and sale of eggs and birds, amounted to *one hundred and fifty pounds a year.*" This gentleman was engaged in a large business requiring much of his time and thought, and it was in answer to a suggestion of a friend of ours, that his poultry must needs pick up much of the profit arising from his bread-winning business, that he produced his "poultry books," and exhibited the above result. Undoubtedly there are many breeders whose returns would show an equally large profit, but the example we quote is a fair specimen of the well-doing of a poultry fancier who has taken up the subject as one from which he derives not only much pleasure, but, as the figures prove, a very fair share of profit also.

It is our intention, in these remarks, to throw together a few practical hints, to assist the efforts of tyros, and spare them, it may be, some cost and trouble upon their entry upon the matter of "poultry fancying," which, like "amateur farming," may become a deep, devouring gulf, in which much money may be swallowed up, with but a shadowy prospect of return, and the poultry-yard become only less costly than training stables, out of which there is nothing turned but "platers" and "outside colts."

Those who are acquainted with such places as Cheltenham or Leamington, will remember the satisfaction with which old Indian officers, who are found in abundance in these localities, will take their visitors round the poultry-yards at the back of Chutney Villa, or Mango Lodge, and point out with pride and triumph their prize cock from Bingley Hall, or their Bantams from Nottingham. These gentlemen are not supposed to make a fair profit, or indeed any profit at all. They are, in the strictest meaning of the term, "fanciers," and indulge their tastes with that lofty disregard for money which is the enviable possession of the wealthy. All goes on well, until some day an exceptional fit of economy takes possession of these "fanciers;" on discovering that their home-bred poultry costs them, perhaps, four or five shillings a pound, they mentally consign their fowls to the furies, and sell their "plant" and stock to some new enterpriser in the same line, and never after carve a chicken at their own table without thinking of the time when the formerly prized "feathered tribe" picked up guineas in the now abandoned poultry-yard.

Now to save a tyro in poultry keeping, or rather poultry-fancying, from disappointment, a little sound and wholesome advice may not be unacceptable, which may enable him to commence the pursuit with a fair prospect of making it moderately profitable; assuming that it is for such, our remarks are designed.

In the first place, in *purchasing* poultry, whether to secure a pen at a show, or at an auction, or to go to dealers and amateurs, is a question necessarily deserving a few words. In a dealer, a good reputation for fairness should be required; and in such a man, with an established reputation for fair dealing, confidence could not reasonably be misplaced; a good price paid to one of this character would be better than laying out less money and getting birds that may turn out worthless.

Auctions are generally thought to be risky sources for obtaining stock, and are now in disrepute. Disease is not unfrequently brought into a healthy yard by means of poultry bought at auctions. An amateur may send surplus stock to be sold by public auction, which, from some cause or other, he would hesitate to offer to private applicants. This is the evil of auctions, which the would-be purchaser has to risk. On the other hand, if the buyer knows a good and healthy bird when he sees it,—and only such men ought to think of purchasing birds there—good bargains and good birds may there often be had. Many people who buy eggs from good birds really do not know the good chickens from the inferior ones; they send their surplus stock to an auction, for the simple reason that they, having no reputation as breeders, cannot privately sell their birds, and they realize more in this way than they would do as table fowls. Thus good birds are often to be picked up at such sales by those who can recognize them in spite of the way in which they are offered for sale, and many well known fanciers at times find this method of disposing of their surplus stock far less troublesome, and just as profitable, all things considered, as selling it to private applicants. Again, that popular journal "The Bazaar," by the security it offers its private advertisers against fraud, is unquestionably an excellent medium for purchasing, disposing, or exchanging, not only eggs and stock, but indeed every other requirement of the poultry yard.

The disadvantage of buying at shows, arises from the fact that the buyer, again, has nothing to rely on but his own eyes and judgment; and, supposing that he secures a pen of fowls, they may have been put together for the identical purpose of selling, but, from *connection*, unfit to mate. Again, from being shut up for many days in an exhibition, they often become roupy and weakened.

From these remarks, then, it will be gathered that in the first place it will not be wise for a man to go with "money in his sack" to the first "crack" poultry show he sees advertised, and buy—even if his means will admit of his so doing—the "first-prize" cock and pair of hens that strikes his fancy, by their points or beauty, regardless of the price marked in the catalogue. The birds are perhaps merely exhibited for that particular occasion, and may be, as we have said, very improperly mated. The pen may, in fact, be "made up" to win a prize, in the same manner as the unsophisticated rustics of a country village, will club together a basket of picked potatoes from several gardens, and thereby "sell" the judges of a cottage garden show, and in the evening divide the prize at the village inn. Alas! that such things should be; but, as the fat knight in "The Merry Wives of Windsor" declares,

"There is naught but roguery in villainous man!"

Apart from this, and assuming that the birds are really what they seem to be, there is still much risk incurred by the purchaser, arising from his want of knowledge as to the means of not only feeding the costly specimens, but of keeping them in good condition when he gets them home.

Should our tyro in poultry breed from his expensive prize-birds, in the event of their being, as we have before suggested, improperly mated, the eggs will fail to produce a continuation of the apparently first-class stock, and should he dispose of the said eggs, he may run the chance of receiving an indignant letter from some customer complaining that he has been "taken in."

A gentleman of our acquaintance once made a purchase of flower roots in Holland, of which the promise ran "that the finest anemones, tulips, and ranuncululi that ever blossomed in an English garden would delight himself and family the following spring." The spring came at last, and with it the Dutchman's flowers came up and blossomed too. But "what a falling off was there" from the previously-formed expectations. Our friend says that he still groans over the lost florins that went into the pocket of that "Rotterdam deceiver!"

So we would say to the beginner, do not "go in" for prize birds without experience; this golden heritage will come to you, as it does to all men, in time; but it is no more inherited than is the power of balancing a straw on the tip of the nose, or making a speech on the Malt Tax.

A man who buys a racer to win a prize therewith, if he succeeds, he simply wins the consequences of his investment. So it is with poultry "honours:" any one with a few pounds in their pockets can buy a prize-gaining bird; but the only *true honour* in such a matter rests with the individual who by care and perseverance *has actually brought that bird to its then present state of perfection*, and through whose means alone it has distanced all its competitors. Poverty may compel such a man, even as it does in every rank of art and industry, "to sell his birth-right for a mess of pottage,"—for the poor man it often is who in the majority of cases, is the genuine fancier;—but the day almost assuredly arrives when, with but comparatively indifferent materials left him to work upon, he finds his "labour of love" requited in the production of a bird equal, if not in fact surpassing, the one he was necessitated to part with, perhaps the season before, *and which carries all before it*. 'Tis said that "money makes the mare to go;" doubtless it does, but here the case is slightly different. Money alone never produces, or ever will produce, a first-class strain; without the necessary skill and ability the cash will be simply wasted and the efforts fruitless.

A tyro is no more able to pronounce on a fowl's value without knowledge and a trained eye than he is capable of distinguishing a cremona from a common fiddle. The man who buys expensive birds from season to season, may keep up a certain amount of continued success; but this kind of success is perfectly well understood by all who "read between the lines." The inferior character of the progeny bred by such persons from even the best birds, mated hap-hazard, brings the whole pursuit into ill favour amongst those who purchase eggs or chickens from such random stock, and who are disappointed in proportion, as their expectations are raised of a first-class variety, by the extravagant prices they have paid for birds of a so-called * "prize strain."

---

* All the facts known to breeders or fanciers tend to diminish very materially the value of any of the specimens so constantly advertised as

Regarding some of the more important details of poultry-fancying, we perhaps cannot do better than again have recourse to "The Illustrated Book of Poultry," and quote the able remarks of its indefatigable author, who, after showing in a particularly lucid manner that no strain of fowl can be brought to anything approaching perfection unless it " be the result of art, care, and study, and even of time," thus continues :—

"It cannot be attained all at once, except by adopting some one else's ready made, and requires a real and steady interest and some perseverance. Without these qualifications it is impossible ever to arrive at it; but assuming the intending fancier to possess them, we will now say how, in our opinion, he ought to proceed. And first, if he have no friend on whose judgment he can rely, but be left entirely to his own resources, the great object for some little time must be not to snatch any sudden success, but to *acquire knowledge,* and more particularly the special knowledge of the particular breed preferred. Such *study of the breed* is the first great essential to success, and should in all cases be commenced at once, every possible show being visited and particular attention being given to the variety in question. This study must be

---

being vaguely of a "prize strain." Taking this expression at its best, and supposing it to be—as it is not always—honestly used, we may take it to mean that certain animals are the product of others which have won a prize: Some one having won at a certain show, advertises eggs, or chickens, or pups, of his "prize strain" and we are frequently asked to give our opinion of the value of such. It is not going beyond the truth to assert that such produce *may* be worth almost any sum; but that it may also be—and is far more likely to be —worth just common market price and no more. And, though this is certainly an extreme case, comparatively seldom to be affirmed, yet still in *some* cases it is the fact, that the worthless specimens may be descended from parents quite equal in value as show specimens to the ancestors of those which are of the highest worth.—" Fancier's Gazette."

thorough and systematic, for it is not only needful to know good birds when they are seen, but to know definitely what makes them superior to others. No breed can thus be "learnt" all at once, though some require much less study than others. The descriptions should be carefully read and mastered, and compared, point by point, with the best specimens to be seen in the show pen.

"Before actually meddling with very expensive stock, it is most desirable to have attained some practical knowledge of fowls and success in their management by real experience with ordinary birds. Where both kinds of knowledge have to be acquired together, we should advise in most cases the purchase, in the first instance, of a few inferior specimens (as regards colour or other matters) from good stock, of the variety to which the preference inclines, which can generally be obtained of good breeders at a small sum. Thus the amateur will gain both the needful experience in management and some practical knowledge of the breed itself at the same time, while such stock after a little may be made highly useful, by comparing first-class specimens with them and training the eye to see *where* the great difference in show value between the two consists. Until some amount of this knowledge be in one way or another acquired, large sums should not be spent upon fowls, if it be desired to avoid serious mistakes and consequent loss. Such a course demands patience, which many perhaps may not feel inclined to bestow; we can only say that very little time need be lost by it, while much useless expenditure may be saved.

"Supposing the taste to have been imbibed, as may probably be the case, at one of the great winter shows, and a few birds to have been thus purchased at a moderate price, we should expect that by March or April some real and *discriminating* knowledge of the breed had been obtained. We would then advise that a few sittings of first-class eggs be procured from sources which can be depended upon, and, if possible, from more than one. The owner's own inferior stock should also to some extent be bred from; and in this way another kind of most valuable and necessary information will be obtained—that of the *appearance of first-class chickens at different ages*, and as compared with inferior ones of the same breed. It must not be assumed that all the chickens from the purchased eggs *are* first-class, for this will not be the case. If birds could be thus bred, their value would cease. The choice specimens are always comparatively few, and, even if one-fourth of any brood are more or less fit for competition, it will be very good indeed. Neither will *all hatch*, except in very rare cases. Highly-bred stock are not quite so fertile, as a rule, and there is some risk in the railway journey. Many chances may even spoil the whole hatch; and if chickens are found dead in the shell, the vendor must not be blamed; since they were *there*, it was not his fault that they did not come to maturity. Out of several sittings, however, there ought to be at least a few really good birds;* and as it will be seen very early that the various little chickens differ greatly in their appearance, careful note should be taken of them, and observation made as to which of them turn out the best at six months old, when they will have assumed their adult plumage. To the fancier with limited space no knowledge is more necessary than this, as it enables him to hatch about three times as many chickens as he can rear, and

---

* Care and time are of course both required in raising good specimens in this manner; but the outlay of money is comparatively small, as eggs from first-rate fowls may often be purchased, new and carefully packed, at prices varying from half-a-guinea to a guinea a setting, which may be relied on; but in this, as in buying stocks at shows or auctions, the integrity of the seller is the only sure dependence.

clear them off at an early period, so as to leave the ground at liberty for the best alone."

Mr. Wright then proceeds in showing how the tyro, by practically studying the good and bad points of any breed, by noting how certain features in the growing chickens are precursors of greater or lesser value, in a purely exhibitional sense, may, in the course of a season, provided "a genuine interest in the subject" be taken, be tolerably competent to judge of a fowl's value, and qualified to purchase really good birds, with every probability of success. In the event, too, of his having "a first-class chicken or two of his own," and which he thinks will bear favourable comparison with those belonging to others, it is suggested that he should exhibit them, discarding, however, any expectation of winning, but really more for the sake of affording him an eligible opportunity of comparing "his own *best* chickens with those from other yards," and thus adding many and important discoveries to his already-existing store of poultry knowledge.

In commencing quite a new strain, the writer again shows the advisability of the tyro having—if his means will allow it—as many "unrelated pens" as possible, as, by these means, a strain is confined within *the limits of his own breeding yard* for a lengthened period; in fact, sufficiently long to define its qualities and put it on a firm basis without the necessity of buying a cock bird every year for "fresh blood," as is frequently advocated. Two advantages at least, it is evident, accrue from this proceeding,—the first being that the tyro can cross his birds with others in his *own* possession, and of whose merits and imperfections *he is already acquainted with*, and by exercising a certain amount of judgment season by season, he, with a greater degree of certainty, attains the summit of his ambition; but if, on the contrary, fresh cock birds are frequently introduced "to recruit" such a strain, "the breeder," as Mr. Wright justly states, " never knows what he is doing, and may spoil all, after years of labour, by an unlucky cross, which brings with it some lurking fault not visible in the bought bird, and therefore never suspected, but which contaminates the whole yard for that year. The danger of this is all the greater from such constant crossing, preventing the home strain from acquiring any strong individual character of its own, which can stand the foreign influence; whereas, if it be carefully bred for some years, the strains of which it was first composed will amalgamate, and it will develope more or less defined features of its own, by which Mr. H.'s strain will by degrees become known to other breeders. It is, in fact, the ideal or standard of the *breeder* which becomes stamped upon it; and as the eye becomes trained to perceive the fine shades of difference, these individual distinctions between various yards are easily recognized, just as the different herds of Shorthorns, all of which arise simply from the ideal standards of perfection as conceived by different breeders."

To those who are really desirous of studying this subject in all its various bearings, we should recommend the perusal of some able articles on "Pedigree Breeding," by the author in question, as it will well repay the reader; but in a small work like the present, space is by far too limited for us to enter into the matter at length. We cannot, however, refrain from subjoining the following excellent extracts from the journal alluded to,* being worthy of special mention, as showing, in a particularly explicit manner, how *all* tendencies and peculiarities are capable of being strengthened or diverted into one definite channel, where skilful breeding is exercised. The writer, it will be noticed, has selected as an example "the fifth toe" as an explanatory medium; but similar reasoning,

---

* The " Fancier's Gazette." Cassell, Petter, and Galpin, Ludgate Hill.

as he remarks, is almost equally applicable to every other point in poultry breeding':—

"It is by no means uncommon for a bird, through some cross with the Dorking of which all traces beside have long since vanished, to appear with some signs of the fifth toe. Though, strictly speaking, this is owing to a tendency inherited long since from the cross, we may for present purposes call it an accidental variation, occurring, perhaps, only twice amongst a thousand chickens supposed to be pure from all Dorking taint. If one of those chickens be bred from it, it is probable that a few of her progeny, but still few, will also show this fifth toe; the greater part, however, reverting to what we may call the usual type of the yard. If we mate this cock to a hen showing a tendency in the same way, the number of five-toed progeny will be somewhat increased; but still (supposing, as we do, that there is no *appreciable* Dorking taint in the yard at all) they will not be many; and the *four-toed* chickens they produced will have little tendency to breed with five toes. But now suppose we select from the chickens produced from these two five-toed parents a pair also five-toed and breed *them* together. We shall now find the tendency vastly increased; so much so, that very likely a full half of the produce will be five-toed, and even those which are not, will show an evident tendency to breed five-toed birds. We have accumulated into one direction—that of producing five toes—the transmitting powers of *two generations*—parents and grandparents. If we breed from this third generation again, still selecting five-toed individuals, the tendency to produce the peculiarity will be increased enormously; and in a generation or two more, a bird *not* five-toed will be as rare as the five-toed specimens originally were. We now have what is called *a strain*, so far as regards this one point of five toes—that is, we have produced a race of birds which we can *depend upon* with almost absolute certainty, to produce nothing but five-toed birds. Such a strain is the Dorking breed itself.

"Now let us put this instance in another light. Supposing the first pair, which showed the feature accidentally, to have been kept alive for ten years, as might easily be the case, whilst their descendants have been successively selected and bred from in the manner supposed. It will readily be seen that it may be very easy to select from the tenth generation a pair of fowls which to the eye appear precisely like the original pair from which operations were commenced. In plumage, in comb, in shape, and in the toes, the closest scrutiny may fail to find any essential difference. But, as we have seen, the difference in breeding value is tremendous. The first pair have scarcely any tendency that can be relied upon to produce the desired five toes; the other pair can be depended upon as regards nearly every one. The first pair presents nothing to a breeder save the foundation upon which he may, by care and perseverance, found a structure hereafter; the other represents work fully done, and a "strain" which, as regards the one point we have considered, is perfected and established, and only needs ordinary care to preserve in the same perfection for an unlimited length of time."

Thus far it will have been seen that poultry-fancying, like a good many other things, presents more or less difficulties in the commencement; but the first steps and the first obstacles once overcome, they clear the way for the onward progress which is in comparison easily attainable. The chief and necessary point, after having partially developed a strain, is in the simple fact of paying due and unceasing care in keeping the breeding stock "up to the mark" by retaining such stock birds as show any particularly desired feature; by so doing both defects and beauties will alike be detected—the one corrected, the other be brought out and still further cultivated. Of course, to effect this perfect beauty of form and feather is not the work of a day, or a series of days: *it is really the work of time and care.* The heterogeneous mixture of the different strains which we have hitherto supposed to have made up our fancier's yard, and the consequent difficulty in making a proper selection for breeding from, will more or less retard his efforts at first; but here again patience and perseverance will have their due reward. Each season will develop fresh beauties and consequently less defects, till little by little, some of the stock will finally gain the *ultimatum* of our fancier's hopes and aspirations by achieving for him not only the honour but the accompanying profits attached to the coveted winner of the first prize or cup. This is the real work to be done, as Mr. Wright has pointed out—"the result not of mere money, but of your patience and skill—and it is work of this kind we wish to encourage and see more of. Merely to win a prize with a bought bird is nothing; but to create a new strain better than all your predecessors is to be of some real benefit, and to be a *real* "poultry fancier."

In stocking a new yard, then, where the experience of poultry fancying is but limited, it is not really important, or in the majority of cases even judicious, to expend any considerable sum in the purchase of "tip top" birds, for the reasons already enumerated. A limited stock of *medium* quality, but descended from a thorough good strain, should really be that sought for, and the endeavour well studied in such stock to counteract existing defects in either sex, by ensuring that the corresponding part in the opposite one is well developed. This will be made clearer as we now proceed to show how the stock should be mated for obtaining such points of excellence as is really desirable.

In breeding for size, regard should be paid to those points which in a table fowl the Houdan should in particular possess, viz., great depth and fulness of breast—the length of the latter bone being very deep in the keel—which should extend prominently from the fore-part towards the tail, that there may be ample room for abundant formation of flesh. Massiveness of body, combined with moderate length, depth, and width, is a great desideratum; large heavy wings and breadth of back are also important points. Thighs should, in addition, be large for flesh purposes, with straight legs, firm and moderately thick, but without a particle of feather.

Provided, however, that the hen be very large, we do not object to a moderate-sized cock, such being as a rule far more active and vigorous than some of the large and heavy birds we have seen exhibited, and which are in fact completely spoilt for brood stock by over-feeding. We have already pointed out one of the most direct consequences of this, and only refer to it again to more particularly impress upon the fancier's mind that the offspring (if any) of over-fed stock-birds invariably result in chickens showing a decided want of stamina. Experience, too, has moreover proved that the future form and size of the chickens are mainly dependent upon the hen. It therefore follows that a largely-developed hen and a compact, closely-built cock are more likely to breed an improved progeny for the point in question than if such proportions were the other way. Indeed the fact seems apparent that while the *frame* is supplied by the hen, the just and proper proportions are filled in by the cock—an example in the economy of nature which may be illustrated by a similar development in other animals, the tall mother, for instance, producing the stalwart son.

In breeding for crest, our experience in mating the parent stock has been this :—We formerly attributed more influence to the cock bird for the reproduction of this feature than to our hens; and as regards cockerels only, see no reason to change our opinion—getting finer-crested young cocks from a hen but mediumly furnished, provided her consort be really good in this respect—than in choosing a full crested hen but an indifferent top-knotted cock; the importance then of a judicious selection in the male bird need scarcely be pointed out.

In pullet-breeding, on the contrary, we would from necessity rather breed from a cock with comparatively hardly a particle of crest, &c., if those of our hens were relatively full and large, than from birds on both sides under the average in this particular. If pullets, then, be the end in view, a full globular crested hen must be depended on, for the more certain realization of the fancier's wishes. If the parents on both sides possess the point advantageously in common, the results naturally will be still more favourable.

In breeding for colour, our own preference lies more towards dark-bodied hens and lighter-plumaged cocks; the progeny from such an union being generally very handsomely marked, cockerels and pullets both, but variable results will at times ensue respecting such. Two seasons back, for example, all our best marked chickens resulted from mating a very dark cock with three particularly light-coloured hens. While, therefore, no rule can be depended upon, it is evident that the sexes should vary in colour; and if a very dark cock bird be used, his hens should be proportionately light, and where, on the other hand, the hens are of darkish plumage, a lighter marked cock should be employed. At present no standard has been formed for "breeding to feather," and which has doubtless tended to keep the real merits of this breed to a greater extent unimpaired than would otherwise have been the case. Provided that show-birds present an uniformity of black and white speckled plumage, is all at present that modern judging requires in this direction.

In breeding for comb, this feature in the cock is important, for we believe his influence is greater than the hens in reproducing it. It should, therefore, in his case, be of good shape and well developed, and, as described in our opening chapter, of the *true Houdan type*. In the hen the endeavour should be to procure it of the precise shape as that of the cock bird, but in miniature. Although the unadvisability of breeding from an ill-shaped combed cock will thus be seen, the comb of a hen may, perhaps, be badly formed, yet, when such a hen is bred from by a cock with a large well-shaped comb, the chicks may not, perhaps, exhibit the objectionable deformity of the mother in the slightest degree.

And so it is really throughout all the points which make up the *ensemble* of real or fancied beauty; the want of such in the hen may be supplied in the chickens if care is taken to select a cock in which they exist, and *vice versa;* but to anticipate any special characteristic to excel in the chickens will prove an unprofitable task, unless one or both of the parents possess it in a minor or major degree.

Supposing, for instance, the birds about to be mated are full grown and handsome, tolerably perfect in all points characterising Houdans *excepting* the crest; if this should be unusually small in both birds, it would be time, trouble, and care merely uselessly expended to breed from them, this being, as we have said, a feature of importance. But if, on the contrary, the hen possessed this desideratum in *perfection,* although the cock's crest might be particularly scanty, we should not only have no hesitation in breeding from them, but, moreover, anticipate some good crested *pullets*.

Or, again, it may be that both cock and hen are creditable specimens of the breed they represent, save that the *fifth* toe in both birds is deficient—(would that "four" toes were the established requirement of judges)—but as custom requires the fifth, its absence under the present standard disqualifies.

Under these circumstances, four-toed birds must naturally be rejected as breeding stock. Or assuming, again, that a hen was fairly good in size and "head gear," yet lighter in colour than could have been desired, and a crooked toe or defective toe-nail unfitted her for showing, she would probably prove a valuable hen for breeding notwithstanding; the faulty toe may have resulted very likely from an accident during chickenhood, and *if* thus originated, would be of no detriment, and the lightness of plumage referred to might be easily compensated by mating, as already shown, with a dark cock.

We might illustrate these facts at greater length; but it is to be hoped that we have succeeded in showing how good birds may, with a little judgment, be bred from parents lacking very essential particulars in the matter of perfection, and be accomplished, too, for a moderate pecuniary outlay only.

The eggs of pullets will occasionally produce very fine chickens; but the general opinion and practice is right, which lay down the rule that the best chickens come from the mating of hens in their second season with two-year old cocks. The chickens that are the offspring of fowls thus mated certainly grow much faster, and we always fancy, in the case of Houdans, are altogether stronger built birds. But it is worth noting that a pen in which cocks are mated with pullets invariably produces a greater number of pullets in a brood than where hens are running with cockerels. Again, cockerels will show a marked preponderance over pullets, particularly during the earlier part of the breeding season, where the male bird is young and vigorous, and the hens are of mature age, but few in number. And again in birds of the same age being put together—no matter whether old or young—the sex of the issue appears uncertain; but if the female portion is not well represented in point of numbers, and the male bird be very vigorous, cockerels will almost for a certainty abound.

CHAPTER V.

ON THE MANAGEMENT OF CHICKENS FOR EXHIBITIVE PURPOSES.

ON entering on this section of our subject, we are directly reminded of the old adage relating to the unwise proceeding of reckoning the interesting little strangers before they are hatched, and this is at once suggestive of a few words both as to the selection of the eggs and the hen we usually look to for the promotion of our desires.

Respecting the eggs, they vary much both in size and colour too, at times; but are generally quite white, with rather a rough-faced shell. Fair average layers appear to produce the largest eggs; very prolific birds those perhaps a trifle smaller, whilst the very smallest and most *unproductive* eggs it has ever been our lot to see have been laid by *highly-bred* adult hens. So long, however, as they are not the product of fat, unhealthy fowls, whether the said eggs be large or small, is not a matter of great import; but for ourselves, we may remark, that if any of the eggs from any favourite hen that we may be desirous of breeding from, present any deviation in shape or size in any considerable degree from those she in ordinary lays, we unhesitatingly reject them.

To ascertain the number of fertile eggs in a batch, no simpler or more effective plan can be adopted than that recommended by Mr. Tegetmier, "of examining them at the expiration of seven or eight days by the aid of a candle, or, still better, a paraffin lamp, and a piece of cardboard, such as the cover of an octavo volume, with an oval cut in the centre not sufficiently large to allow an egg to pass through. The cardboard is held near the light, and the egg to be examined placed against the opening. After being sat upon for a week the fertile eggs are always opaque, excepting at the larger end where the air-vesicle exists, and the sterile eggs are readily distinguished by the adjective *clear* which is usually applied to them. A little practice renders the distinction easy. The clear eggs being removed, more room remains for those that are fertile, and they receive a greater amount of warmth."

Disappointing results in hatching frequently ensue from the non-observance of the most simple precautions; the freshness of the eggs, limitation as to number, and the condition of the hen previous to the commencement of her duties, are among the most prominent of the shoals and quicksands on which so many a young fancier's hopes and expectations are wrecked. We prefer those eggs which have not been laid more than a fortnight. The number is more or less dependent on the size of the hen; but as we prefer smallish hens ourselves, we therefore limit the batch to nine, and early in the year to seven eggs at most. We make sure the hen in question is *really* broody, and not apparently so, and therefore give her three or four hard-boiled eggs to sit upon for a couple of days, to test her in this respect before we risk a valuable batch. We never attempt to set a hen without due examination, and if any signs of uncleanliness prevail; we adopt the treatment we have recommended in p. 64. A damp spot is generally acknowledged as the best suited for hatching, but we have had as many, if not more, chickens from "high level" nests as upon the ground. When we adopted the former expedient, a layer of damp earth, four or five inches thick, formed the basis of the nest; on this we put a freshly-cut turf slightly hollowed; in very early spring we covered this lightly over with hay, but substituted straw of short lengths if the weather was at all mild, afterwards sprinkling the whole well with manganeze or black sulphur. If, after setting for a fortnight, and the weather happened to be dry and warm, we removed our hen at night—she being then quiet—and poured a tumbler full of warm water over both eggs and nest, and then carefully replaced her; we have also found it advisable to repeat this about forty-eight hours before hatching was due. Such was our usual *modus operandi*, and we were generally rewarded with good batches; but for the future we hope to be less reliant upon our hens than we have done hitherto. For many breeders now find it far more advantageous to their interests to employ artificial means for incubation, time being, as they aver, in the first place better utilized, besides the avoidance of waste of flesh and strength incurred by the hens while sitting. If such results can be satisfactorily depended upon, the value of incubators for hatching—not only the eggs of Houdans, but those of all non-sitting breeds—is at once apparent, and worthy of a passing remark.

Although there is nothing new in the idea—chickens being hatched by various artificial processes in an age long gone by, before even such men as Aristotle, Pliny, and others lived and flourished—it is only within the past few years comparatively that fanciers have given this subject any considerable degree of attention. Coming back, however, with a bound to a more recent period than the Roman era, since M. Réaumer, who we believe, was the first European experimentalist in this direction—several eminent names, amongst which Cantello, Bonnemain, Carbounier, and others figure prominently in having devised, altered, and improved upon the efforts of their predecessors. In a like manner, more modern appliances still have formed the subjects for a vast amount of thought, skill, and ingenuity on the part of various manufacturers; and at the present time there are several machines which are ascribed as being more or less efficient in action. Amongst these may be enumerated one of a very simple character, but to which nevertheless its inventor, Mr. Crook, has devoted many years care and attention, and represented by Fig. 10, which appears, judging from the remarks and experiments of Mr. Wren, of Lowestoft, to carry out the object of its inventor, in a far higher degree than any other, being apparently the only one in which *actual success* has been achieved. The comparative failure of nearly all incubators hitherto introduced appear to have originated chiefly in a *want* of proper and through ventilation, such as is afforded to the eggs *through the feathers of the sitting hen* by every movement of her body, and this drawback at length seems to have been—or is now in a very fair way, at all events, of being—remedied by a *continuous supply of fresh air* being artificially provided for.

Fig. 10.

Owing to this important condition being overlooked, simple as were the rules enjoined for ensuring success in the abstract, in actual *working*, unless in very experienced hands, disappointment was not the exception, but the invariable rule; for this reason—our own experience of incubators having been rather of an unsatisfactory character—we have given our preference to hens, setting two or more at one time, transferring the chickens when hatched to one hen, and a fresh complement of eggs to another, as already described in page

34, but we must candidly admit that *later experiments* have convinced us that if incubators are not to be relied on for the *entire* fulfilment of the ordinary duties of a sitting hen, they can at least be made particularly serviceable *in completing what she has already begun*, and which some remarks by Mr. Halsted, who has also investigated the subject of artificial incubation at great length, will at once make apparent. He writes as follows in the American "Standard of Excellence:"—

"Set your eggs under the hen, and at any time after ten days incubation remove them to the machine. You can then put another setting of eggs under the hen; in fact, three or four sittings in succession will not injure her. By this process your eggs are almost certain to hatch, your chicks come out strong and healthy, free from vermin and disease, none are trod to death in the nest, and none are left by the hen and chilled before fairly dry."

We consider that it scarcely falls within our province to dilate in any way upon the working details of hatching by artificial means—although admitting its importance—firstly, from the very narrow compass in which our task is necessarily confined, and that full instructions for management can be obtained from the manufacturer—and, secondly, that in "Land and Water," the *secret* of success is, for the first time described, in a series of talented articles on "The Art of Artificial Incubation," and to which our readers should refer.

Providing, however, that incubators and artificial rearing appliances—respecting which we shall have occasion presently to say a few words—are, by our fancier not brought into requisition, when the eggs are all hatched, or as many as are likely to do so, the hen and chickens should be cooped in such a shed as we have before described if early in the season; but if the weather be favourable, *i.e.*, warm and dry, the coop may then with advantage be placed out of doors upon dry gravelly ground. The form of coop is a question hardly worth discussing, and there are, moreover, plenty to choose from. The one already alluded to (Fig. 7) with a hinged board for shelter, as suggested, is well adapted; also the triangular one seen in Fig. 11, with a wire run for the protection of the chickens, and which can be obtained complete for a few shillings. A more elaborate and useful contrivance, again, is represented by Fig. 12, such being constructed entirely of galvanized and japanned iron, and therefore very durable. Its usefulness speaks or itself. On a grass run, thus confined, the chickens are safe from cats or rats, and can run to the hen mother to be brooded when they require it.

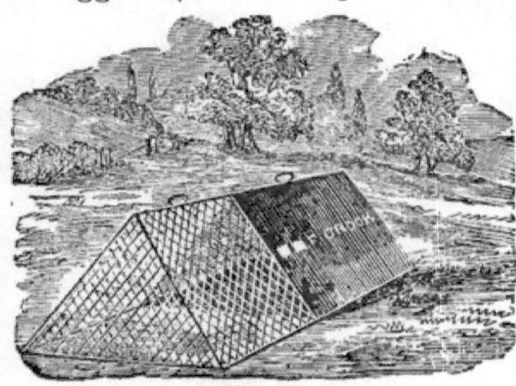

Fig. 11.

Perhaps, however, one of the most complete and efficient hen coops and chicken protectors that we have yet seen is the Portable Game and Poultry Coop, depicted in Fig. 13, manufactured by Mr. E. Lloyd, of the Horticultural Works, Grantham, Lincolnshire. These useful contrivances are made in sizes varying from six feet long by two or three feet wide to twelve feet long by six feet wide if required. One end is covered as a protection against inclement weather, and the rest panelled with galvanized iron wire netting, removable at pleasure. Small wheels are easily attached, so that these houses can be shifted daily to fresh ground with the utmost ease. For the convenience of transit, all can be taken to pieces, packed in a very small compass, and put together again by almost any person. Unlike most poultry coops, these can

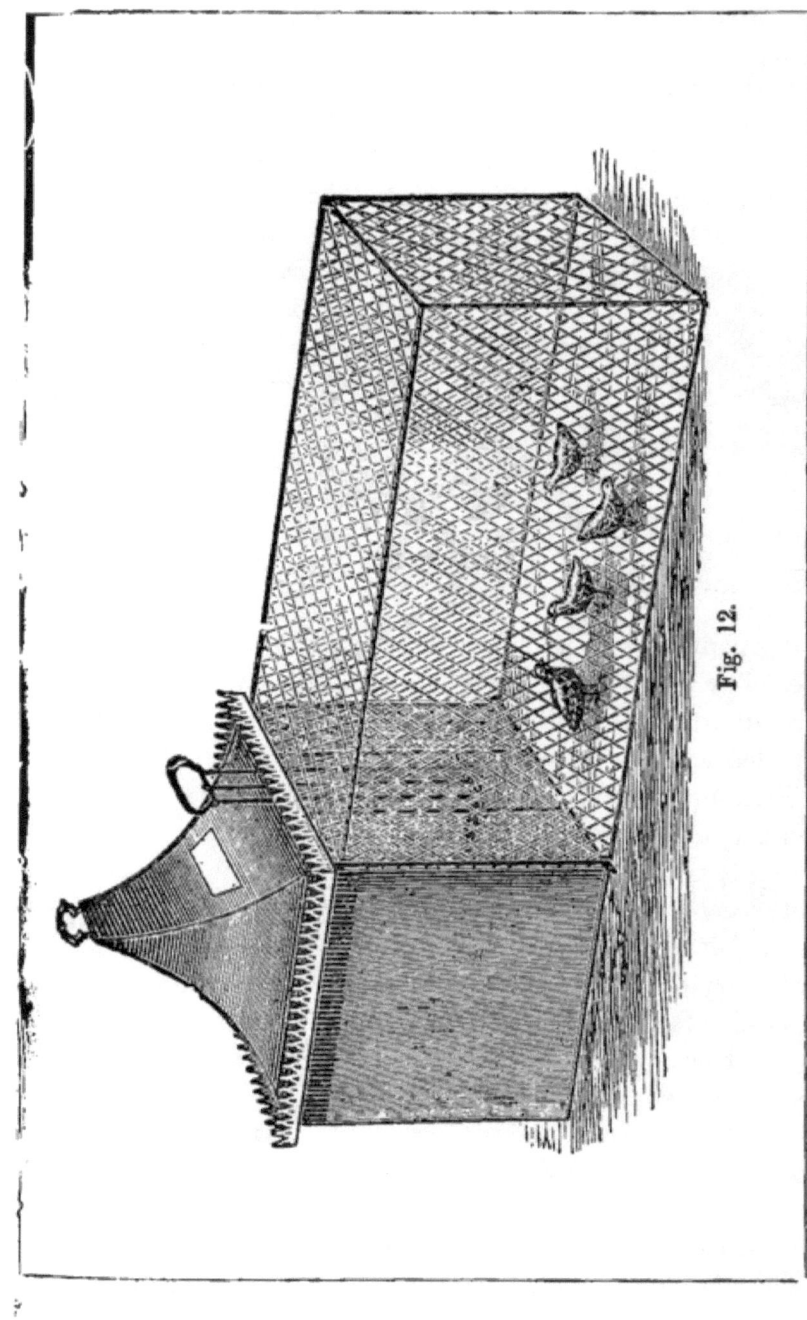

Fig. 12.

EARLY DISTINGUISHING SIGNS OF THE SEX. 109

be utilised nearly all the year round, as, by simply substituting glass for the iron in the panels, they form the prettiest miniature greenhouses it is possible to conceive. They are, in fact, as useful for all practical purposes as they are ornamental in appearance or moderate in price.

The great rapidity with which the chickens fledge has always been a matter of surprise, but it shows the necessity of good and nutritious feeding until the process is completed, so as to compensate for the unusual call upon the system. It seems a remarkable fact, however, that, unlike most of the fast-feathering breeds, the Houdan appears to undergo fewer draw-

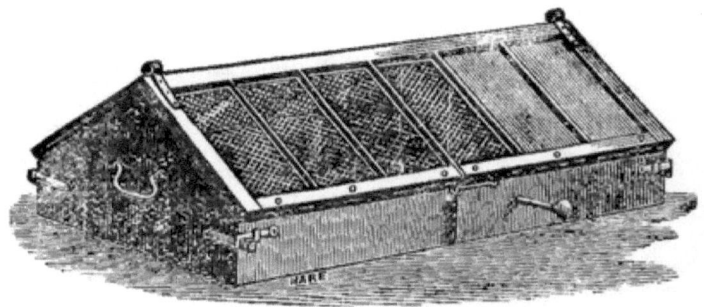

Fig. 13.

backs in this respect than any other class of fowl we are acquainted with. The day following they are hatched, the wing feathers are visible, and feathering proceeds at such an amazing rate, that at an age when chickens of other breeds are still in their furry down, the Houdan is all but fully feathered. The sex can be distinguished at a very early age by the combs, the cockerels speedily showing it, whilst the pullets will very frequently not have the slightest indication of it until their adult plumage is complete; moreover, the wing feathers of the cockerels, as in most breeds, are more pointed than those of the pullets, the latter being rounder and wider.

H

They are pretty little creatures when first hatched in their black and lemon-coloured furry garb, and one of the principal tests as to their probable future value as show birds is soon made known as regards "crest," by the size of the small projecting poll of fluff, the extent of this determining the future amount of crest the bird will possess when fully grown, for in proportion to the size of this projection, so will the crest be fully or imperfectly developed in the adult bird. This in a measure also applies to the muffling.

In now treating of the chickens we have assumed that they *are* of the better class, and therefore that any trivial addition to the ordinary cost of feeding will not be grudged. To rear them to the greatest size is the point in question, and for this object there cannot be a better kind of food employed than grass or lettuce cut very small, dry bread well crumbled, and course oatmeal in equal parts, with half a part of bone-meal *

---

* This useful addendum to chicken-feeding, bone meal, can be obtained from Ellis & Sons of the Sparkenhoe Manure Works, Leicester, at a very moderate cost. Its valuable properties are now generally acknowledged, for it is without doubt one of the greatest desiderata in the feeding of poultry. We quite agree with others that, used with discretion, it certainly not only tends to prevent hens from laying soft or shelless eggs, but enhances the redness of their combs and gives to their plumage a far more brilliant appearance. We have, moreover, given it as our opinion, in page 62, and in this opinion are supported by Mr. F. Crook, whose poultry experience needs no comment from us, that by its judicious usage the hens will not be so much addicted to eat each others feathers, frequently observable in very small yards; this peculiar habit we have opined, arising from a craving induced by such confinement or artificial treatment in which, as we have said, they cannot procure that material "bone meal," so amply and so successfully seems to supply them with; for this evil is not observable in either game or poultry raised in a semi-wild state, and who doubtless provide themselves with some animal substance, which the bone meal is intended to substitute in the case of poultry reared entirely under artificial conditions. In addition to the advantages already claimed by the use of bone meal, Mr. Wright, in his little work on "The Brahma" states, "that there is a marked difference both in the size and stamina of birds reared with it over others.

added, the whole to be mixed to a proper consistence with new milk; the bread, which may be less freely used as the youngsters grow older, is a good medium for absorbing the milk and giving just the crumbly consistence to the food that is required. Oatmeal should not be used alone, as the chicks often tire of it, and it is, when unmixed with the chopped grass and bread, too heating. More milk may be used after two months, and then barley-meal and toppings may be used instead, or "Spratt's Poultry Food," if it is found that oatmeal palls upon the appetite; but the bread and bone meal should form a part of the food, and which should be so mixed with the milk that it crumbles easily. When but a day old, food should be given every two hours; later, every three hours will do; but so long as the chickens seem really hungry, the intervals of feeding should not be very extended. This particular care, both in a dietary and systematical sense, *must* be taken when "size" is the object to be gained; smaller birds, but still very good ones, may be reared with less strict attention. Twice daily, in addition to their food, milk should be given; all young animals appreciate it, and it greatly assists their development, particularly if hatched early in the year; but in very hot weather, or after a course of seven or eight weeks, it should be abandoned; crushed hempseed we have also found a very useful auxiliary to chickens food when cold weather prevails. Chopped grain of some kind—we prefer grits—should form the last meal at night; but after

---

It adds to the size of the birds; it postpones their maturity, or 'setting' as poultrymen call it, after which growth nearly ceases; it greatly prevents leg-weakness in the cockerels; and it tends to produce full and profuse feathering, and to assist in fledging. Burnt bones, or phosphate of lime, have not the same effect by any means; and raw bones crushed have the fault of inducing early laying in the pullets, whereas the bone dust rather postpones it."

they are a week or ten days old, canary seed, hempseed, or buckwheat may be given whole From the middle of winter up to early spring, this last meal should be given them as late at night as possible; and if thus fed as recommended, the grain will take longer in digesting, and thus afford their little bodies a greater amount of heat. Toast and ale was a very favourite food with us at one period; but our later experience has shown us that Houdans are none the worse for being "Good Templars" of the feathered tribe; a little meat, however, once a day, or "Spratt's Granulated Crissel." we have, on the other hand, found particularly serviceable in bringing them on.

During the earlier period of chickenhood, as a means to prevent waste, we have very successfully made use of a feeding cage like, the one seen in Fig. 14, and where expensive food, as it frequently is, is far from an unimportant item in a fancier's expenditure, its utility is apparent. An unlimited supply of green food is absolutely essential to all chickens that are bred in confinement; cut up fine with a sharp knife, or shears, they will take it eagerly, and in fact eat more of it too, than if they had a grass run, when this trouble would not of course be necessary.

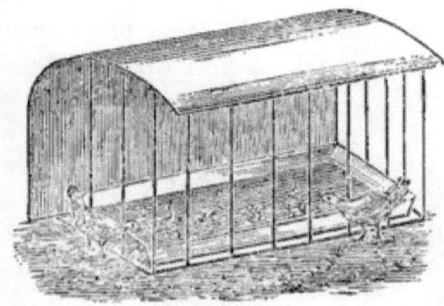
Fig. 14.

There are possibly but few well-established poultry-yards in the present day in which "iron solution" is not used, and thanks to Mr. J. Douglas—who, we believe, was the first to make its useful properties generally known—several complaints incidental and formerly prevalent amongst fowls are now comparative strangers. It is simply made thus :—the ingredients being

    Sulphate of Iron .... 1lb.
    Sulphuric Acid .... 1oz.

These are dissolved in a jug of hot water capable of holding a quart, and allowed to remain undisturbed for four-and-twenty hours. It should then be added to a gallon of spring water, and bottled for use. The dose being a teaspoon full to every pint of the water in the drinking vessels, every other day for chickens, and once or twice a week for the adult stock. During the moulting season it should be always used. It is a fine tonic, and one of the best *preventatives* of disease.

When the mother begins to "shake off" the chickens, they should be moved to fresh ground, their late quarters being thus utilized for a younger brood if necessary. There is no doubt that the growing chickens do best where each brood can be accommodated with a separate house and run; but it very frequently happens that the amount of room this necessitates is not at the disposal of the owner, and in this case

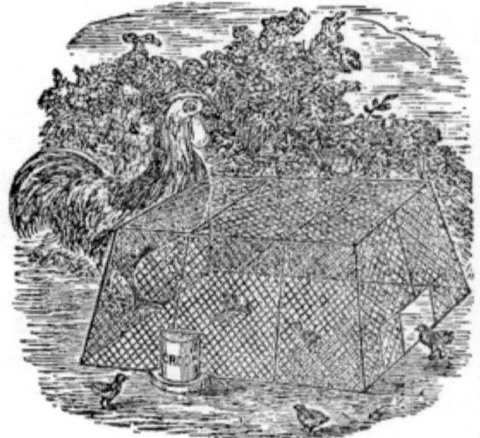

Fig. 15.

chickens of about the same age will do better when put together than if they vary much in this particular. But if from want of accommodation, chickens of different ages are unavoidably compelled to be fed together in the open yard, the older ones will tyrannize over their younger companions and gorge themselves with food, while the lesser ones will for a certainty " go short " unless some provision be made that *all* enjoy their proper modicum. This is most effectually provided for by using the 'lattice chicken folds,' as represented by Figs. 15, 16, 17, for it will be seen that chickens of different sizes are thus enabled to have their due share without being disturbed, or driven about by older birds in their quest of it.

Fig. 16.

When the runs are extensive, planting shrubs in them is highly advisable; they give shade to the birds, and have also a pretty appearance. Another excellent method is to plant, towards April, various sorts of cabbages in a portion of the run set apart for that purpose. This cabbage plantation will be found of great advantage when chickens of three or four months old, or even older, are turned into it.

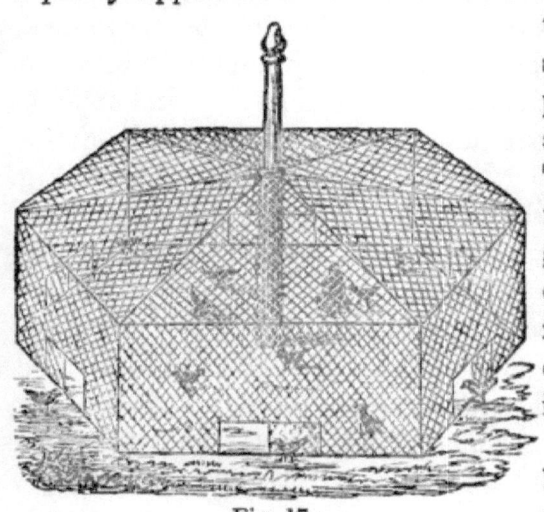

Fig. 17.

Chickens should not be permitted to perch too soon, or crooked breasts will in all probability be the result. This peculiarity is really caused by the reason of their being so profitable; the more profitable the more they are liable to it, for they put on flesh very rapidly, more rapidly at times than they form stout bone to carry it, and consequently the tender cartilage is bent or twisted by the weight it has to bear when the chicken is on the perch. It is not often that a disfigurement equally affects a bird reared for exhibition and for the table, but it is so with this defect; in fact, it is more unsightly when the fowl is trussed and dressed than when it is alive, for then it needs to be examined and handled before this malformation is disclosed. This is a serious defect in the prize pen, and certainly an unsightly one at the dinner table.

The best way to prevent it is the daily use of the bone meal already alluded to, and to litter the young chickens, as is done with a lot of young pigs. Upon a *dry* floor covered with sifted earth, put a good litter of short straw; the straw should be daily lifted and shaken, and all uncleanliness removed. Or dry ashes, if preferred, about a couple of inches in depth, can be substituted; but they should be taken away every morning and replaced by a fresh supply. Either of these plans will keep the chickens warm all day, and at night —when the temperature is colder—an "artificial" mother affords a capital means of guarding against its effects. Fig. 18 shows a really useful rearing apparatus of this description, which will prove of infinite value in bringing up the young stock without the services of a hen at all, if so desired, the necessary heat being very simply afforded by a water vessel and lamp. It is no use to have the chickens warm at night, if during the day, they are exposed to chills; they should have extra means of warmth during the hours when the greater degree of cold exists; in the artificial mother, huddled together, they get this additional warmth; and if light screens are placed in front of the runs, as suggested in page 29, such an emergency is at once provided for.

Indeed, when poultry operations are extensively conducted, and it is intended to raise a large proportion of chickens with comparatively few hens, we quite agree with Mr. W. M. Lewis, for it is now *practically* corroborated " that they can be just as well reared—and in some cases even better—by artificial than by the natural method. The only use of the hen," as he observes, " is to prevent the natural heat of the chick's body from cooling—to break up the food, and protect them from danger. In fact, chickens do not really require a hen. They only require a suitable covering for their bodies until full-fledged to preserve their natural heat, so as to keep their bodies warm the same as full-grown fowls.

" The artificial mother is very convenient to persons raising poultry, either on a large or small scale, to get early chickens in January or February, when the weather will not permit them to run out, and to have fine large fowls for exhibition in the fall months. For large poultry-dealers a good light house is required, with good ventilation, without a draught; a dry and well-gravelled floor; sun-light, and a small run, with a little fire, in very cold, damp, chilly, and rainy days, to keep the atmosphere dry, is all that is needed to raise as fine chickens as may be desired. The artificial mother, however, is a great economizer of time and labour—saves the necessity of any coops which would otherwise be needed. It protects the little chicks from the changeableness of the weather; and by this mode they are also completely under control, and where they can be given all sorts of nourishing drinks and food without fear or trouble from the mother hen."

Mr. Crook, the inventor of the apparatus of which we have given an illustration, further claims that " the young chicks, artificially reared, are not subject to so many risks as when the hen is with them; they are not liable to be called into danger nor into wet places. The only thing required is a little extra watching to feed and provide for them as near to nature as possible, and they will thrive with every appearance of natural means having been employed, and with full reward for the little extra attention bestowed upon them."

To get fine birds, the cockerels, at eight or nine weeks old, should be separated from the pullets, or, from their vigorous propensities, they will attain maturity too soon, notwithstanding all the trouble that may be bestowed to get them large and well proportioned.

At this time, or within a week or two later at most, the whole of the youngsters should be well scanned, and all but

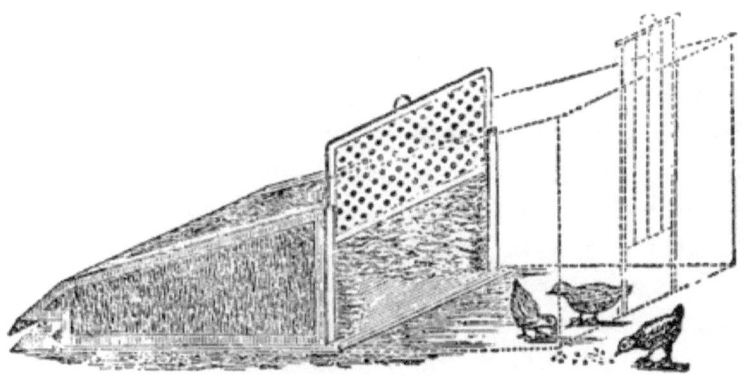

Fig. 18.

the really promising ones disposed of; twisted or fallen crests, deficiency or deformity of the toes, crooked backs or beaks, will, of course, preclude any idea of prize-winning; but a scantiness of beard at this age, in comparison with the crest, is very common, the chickens being sometimes three parts fledged ere the beard developes itself in the cockerels to any considerable degree; also, if bred from well-marked, darkish birds, no chicken, if otherwise good, should be slightingly passed over for presenting a rather light appearance at this period, for although, after their first moult, the adult fowls certainly *do* get lighter coloured, the chickens, on the contrary, will get considerably darker as they get older. But if the semi-Crêve-cœur type (alluded to in our opening chapter) is to gain still further ascendancy (we now speak of colour only) we must then coincide with Mr. R. B. Wood, that pullets and cockerels both, must be very dark indeed to make good-coloured birds in after years; and, further, that although such birds may be too dark for immediate competition, they may, neverthless, provided they are good in other respects, be useful for showing or breeding at a future time.

In fine seasons, early-hatched pullets, fed as we have recommended, will almost for a certainty lay at about five months old; and to prevent it, is at times difficult, the increasing warmth of the year developing all animal growth and fecundity in a wonderful manner; meat, in any form, should not be given at this time to either sex; it will cause a premature enlargement of the combs of the young cocks, and give the pullets a direct tendency to carry out nature's dictates too early for the attainment of that "large" size so desired, but bone-meal should still be used. When the combs of the pullets become enlarged and red, thereby exhibiting a sign that may lead one to suspect in them a tendency to lay, they should be shifted to fresh quarters as soon as possible. Changing their runs, in most cases, has the effect, for a short period generally, of checking the instinct; indeed, by its studied repetition, some breeders have thus put off for *several weeks* its actual fulfilment,—but to the fowl's depreciation after, we must add, more or less in its value as an egg-producer. In moderation, and begun at a comparatively earlier period—say when they are about fifteen or sixteen weeks old—not quite so much harm is, perhaps, done to their future laying prospects by shifting them about from run to run every two or three weeks; and laying may be thus postponed even in early-hatched birds considerably beyond the usual time.

From some remarks made by Mr. T. Waterman, in the "Fancier's Gazette," we gather that of a brood of chickens hatched in January three in the following May began to lay; seeing this, he at once transferred the remainder to a different pen, and gave them the following food, viz., equal proportions of barley meal and sharps in the morning—but rather limited as to quantity—and, with the exception of green food, represented by a suspended cabbage, and of good heavy barley, one feed, and that about three o'clock in the afternoon, was all they received till the following morning. But this alteration of diet and run procured in a measure the result he aimed at, their *baby-like appearance being maintained, and growth proceeding rapidly*. Sharps, barley-meal, boiled meat minced and incorporated with a slight seasoning of ground carraway seeds and cut grass with crushed oyster shells, was the previous course of feeding he had adopted. The roosting houses of the pullets subjected to the altered treatment, he adds, "were quite open in front and ends, so as to be as cold as possible for the season of the year." He gives it as his opinion (and one, moreover, in which we perfectly concur) that "warm housing promotes laying quite as much as diet;" he recommends the above as being "the best method for retarding the laying of young pullets, and finds it succeed by removing them to another pen every month."

In thus briefly pointing out what latitude can be given in this direction, we must candidly admit that the practice is considerably deteriorating the "laying" qualities not only of Houdans, but most other breeds; and so long as this really valuble instinct is sacrificed for mere beauty of form and feather, we are afraid there will be little chance of improvement in this respect, unless it be whilst the one class of poultry breeders are directing their energies to the furtherance of certain points of a "fancy" value, others encourage and endeavour to *improve* the laying instincts as suggested in a previous chapter.

We have found that the chickens certainly get in finer condition with a wide range; but the worst of it is they mature far too rapidly to make large exhibition fowls. Confinement, on the contrary, and want of sufficient exercise, although productive of size, if appropriate feeding is combined, tell to a certain extent upon the carriage of the birds, which from this cause is, perhaps, not quite so sprightly as is seen in other chickens that have been allowed more latitude in their bringing up. It follows, therefore, that runs of *medium* extent, just sufficiently large to ensure a constant plentitude of green food, and no larger, affords the best facilities after all; they, moreover, are conducive to that *regularity of feeding* we have already alluded to, and which is so essential, but which it is almost impossible to carry out where the range is very extensive.

As sad havoc is at times made not only with food, but eggs and chickens likewise, by rats and cats, a few simple hints to obviate this and set these unwelcome visitors at defiance deserve attention. A correspondent to the "Poultry Bulletin," who, it appears, suffered considerably by the food in his poultry-houses being eaten by rats, after trying many unsuccessful experiments, at length devised the following simple expedient, which he remarks "may be as old as the hills to many readers," but it was new to him, and may be to many others who would like to profit by his experience:—

"Take a round tin pan, punch three holes at equal distances near the rim, and fasten a piece of wire or cord, about fifteen inches long, in each hole; secure the ends together, and attach them to a single cord, and suspend the pan from the ceiling of your poultry-house so that the bottom of it is about six inches from the ground. Your fowls can easily eat out of the pan; but the rats are unable to, on account of the swinging motion, the pan giving away as soon as they touch it. It is, of course, necessary to suspend the feeding trough or pan, which ever you like to call it, clear of any boxes or anything from which the rats can get into it."

Poison is undoubtedly the best safeguard against rats—and many writers aver for "cats" too—but as we are no advocates for unnecessary slaughter, we are of opinion that other means may be found that are quite as effectual. Of the former class of intruders we are happy to say we have been hitherto free, and, as regards the latter, we may observe that we never give them a chance of harming our young stock, the latter being too well protected. In other yards we have known a piece of wood saturated with valerian oil and Battle's Vermin Killer well incorporated with a piece of meat, and attached to the wood, to be thoroughly efficacious for rats. The wood is to be placed in a rat run, properly secured, and, need we say, wholly beyond the reach of the hens. Rats are not bad judges of some of the good things of this life. To eggs, in particular, they evince a strong partiality; and, as it has been known that even those under a setting hen have with impunity been abstracted by them, it of course is not surprising that where readier access is obtained—such as to the ordinary laying nests—the eggs will at times rapidly disappear if not collected very frequently.

Several methods have been suggested for checking Pussy's depredations, but to be really effectual involve more or less cruelty. The two following plans, given by a correspondent in the "Fancier's Gazette," are not, however, quite so open to this objection; they appear to have been successful, and, therefore, worth repeating, and, moreover, a fancier by these means incurs no risk of being brought within the clutches of the law. He writes thus :—

"I discovered a notorious 'chicken-eater' concealed in a hamper, quite close to the 'run,' quietly contemplating the chance of a plump chicken for dinner. I immediately procured a bucket of cold water, and treated the depredator to a cold bath, which had such an effect on his nervous system that he never attempted to come near the chickens again. In justice to Miss Watts, the celebrated breeder of fowls, I must say that it was through her that I heard of the experiment. I think if some of your readers would try the cold water cure when trapped, they will find it act successfully, as I have proved.

"Another experiment. I secured our house cat close to the young chicks, placing one within easy reach of the cat. When I found the cat inclined to pounce upon the chick, I applied a thin switch to his sides, and, after treating him to the rod two or three times, I allowed him to move about with the chickens. He soon became reconciled, and now moves about amongst them, never attempting to molest them."

Eggs from first-class brood stock being of considerably greater value during the early period of the year—either for selling or home sitting—than later on, it is a matter of no small importance to consider how they can be best ensured. It was our intention to have animadverted on this subject at the close of the preceding chapter, but a few words in concluding the present one relating thereto may we think with due propriety be admitted. At first sight, this object would appear to be very easily accomplished, as in September, at the very latest, early-hatched pullets will prove productive if special means, as already pointed out, are not taken to *prevent* it. But from what we have elsewhere stated, it will be gathered that their eggs are not quite so well adapted for hatching purposes as those from mature hens. We said in page 49 that it was not at all uncommon for the hens, during the latter part of the season, to occasionally evince a broody tendency; and we also there further mentioned our *reason* for encouraging it, when the birds were of value,—as the reader will perceive by referring to the page in question,—for nothing will facilitate the object here in view more than this. But as it happens that the larger proportion of the hens of this breed never take to the nest excepting for the purpose of depositing a more or less valuable product,—keeping on laying in fact for an indefinite period if fed to this end,—our suggestion in this case is in no way applicable, for they would be *leaving off* at the very time their eggs were most wanted.

As then, in the instance of pullets, a somewhat similar course of treatment must be carried out as the autumn approaches, keeping them from the cock bird until three weeks or a month before their eggs are wanted, frequent changes of run being resorted to, and every kind of stimulating diet unflinchingly withheld. By these means there will be a moderate proportion of fertile eggs which can be depended upon when most required. We have said a moderate proportion, because a *very* large number on which reliance can be really placed in the very early season can scarcely be expected. For, notwithstanding the admitted vigorous nature of the Houdan cock, an older bird of any breed, as a rule in cold weather, will fail to impart that fertility to the egg which may be expected in a younger compeer; but much may be done to produce it by special feeding, not only while separately confined, but after the breeding pen is made up for the season. The moderate use of stimulants and tonics as accessories to the ordinary diet will now prove particularly serviceable; but these must at all times be regulated according to the condition of the fowls and the state of the weather. There is no harm, however, in giving animal food daily, and while the *occasional* use of condiments cannot but prove advantageous, their continual use is to be condemned.

Perhaps one of the most useful prescriptions for the indentical purpose we are now considering is the following:—

Gentian Root	1oz.
Carbonate of Iron	4oz.
Sulphate of Quinine	1oz.
Aniseed	1oz.
Cayenne	1oz.

These ingredients must be all finely powdered and thoroughly mixed, and kept in a stoppered bottle for use; this formula being, perhaps, a somewhat expensive one, a lesser quantity can be made up if desired, care being taken to observe the above proportions. For use, just a sufficiency should be added to the morning meal of soft food to flavour it, but not to impregnate it too strongly.

CHAPTER VI.

SUGGESTIONS ON EXHIBITING.

AS October approaches, and shows follow one another thick and fast, ere our fancier launches his bark upon the deceptive waters of prize-poultry competition, a few hints may not prove unacceptable as a guide to the haven of success. For however good birds may be, as remarked by Mr. W. H. Nichols, "they all require more or less attention in preparing them for the show-pen. No one who keeps race-horses, and who had any expectation of winning, would send an untrained horse to run in a race, neither will an experienced exhibitor send his birds to a show without first preparing them."

When showing, then, is really decided upon, a rather higher, and more liberal class of feeding than we have hitherto advocated, is in the first place usually found more or less necessary; therefore daily, for a week or two preceding exhibition, stimulating diet, such as linseed jelly, meat, hempseed, &c., are frequently given with the ordinary food, such ingredients adding considerably to the "plumpness" of the birds, and to the lustre of their plumage; but excess should be strictly avoided; and no approach to fattening be allowed. In the case of cockerels only, the daily use of raw crushed bones meet with favour at the hands of several of our well-known exhibitors; and from their gelatinous composition they certainly facilitate full and profuse feathering; but a friend of ours, when congratulated two seasons back at the "Palace" show upon the splendid condition of a cockerel, told us afterwards in confidence (there is no harm in now divulging it, as, poor fellow, he has "gone the way of all flesh") that he was indebted for the result to several extensive repasts of crushed "snails" he had regaled the bird with for the previous month." Such diet, however—we are speaking now of raw bones—beneficial as it may be for the cockerels or the older male birds, should be very cautiously used where pullets or hens are concerned, all stimulating food having a tendency to produce inflammation of the egg-organs. Sulphate of iron solution gives a great brilliancy to the comb and plumage, and also that *tone* usually expected in a first-class cup-winner. These auxiliaries should therefore not be lost sight of in getting birds ready for exhibition.

Where the fowls are kept on a large range, or in the case of newly-purchased ones to test their merits, or restrain their wildness, we advise the fancier having a shed at disposal, and therein to form a few pens—this a week or so before the intended exhibition will be found in every way almost necessary. These pens should be placed from three to four feet from the ground, and be of different sizes, according to the size of the birds. Each pen should be fitted with a wire front; in such they (the birds) may be kept perfectly safe for some considerable time, if so desired, soft food, grass, small gravel and water being of course requisite. The advantage of such pens, moreover, are, that the intending exhibitor can thus compare his best birds not only leisurely and quietly, but thoroughly scrutinize them, point by point, before he absolutely determines which *is* the best; for this is not always the easy matter which anyone unacquainted with the matter would suppose, and, in the present day, owing to the excellent standard to which show birds are, as a rule, now brought, it is simply cost and trouble uselessly expended to send off any *but the best* with a view to prize-taking.

Tameness, in all intended exhibition birds, should be encouraged by every possible means. How frequently really good specimens are passed over by a judge simply because, they, being of a wild or timorous nature, crouch into corners, and look their "worst," instead of their "best," many an exhibitor knows but two well; whereas a tame bird will stand bolt upright and defiant, in front of the pen, appearing only too pleased to court observation. We therefore maintain that any treatment conducive to such results should not be lost sight of. "If they can be kept for a time in a yard by the house" remarks Miss Watts, "where crumbs and scraps from the table are thrown out, and where they can have notice from children and other members of the family, the familiar tameness they will acquire will tell well in their looks in the exhibition pen, where the scared look of a wild fowl, or the self-possessed, quiet demeanour of a tame one, makes a great difference."

As a good method of preparing choice cockerels for the ordeal of exhibition, it has been suggested to place them, like younger school-boys under the ken of a superior and older monitor, who by his influence can keep the youngsters under surveillance. To any one observant of the manners and habits of poultry, this domineering spirit of the older cocks is naturally familiar, and forms an excellent discipline for training the younger birds previous to their entrée into "female" society. Nature is nature all over the world, and as a boy is ever proud of being flirted with by the opposite sex, so likewise we see how young male animals, and birds particularly, strut and plume themselves when placed in consort with females of the same class. To those who have regarded the consequential bearing of a young cock subjected to the delicate attentions of two or three wide-awake hens, this must have been plainly obvious, and has led more than one successful breeder to pursue this plan of placing — some few weeks before the intended exhibition—a promising cockerel with one or two hens, thereby bringing him out *with no mean opinion of himself*, so that when he appears at the show he will, after the previous treatment, exhibit his quality and style to the greatest perfection.

Valuable birds are frequently unfitted for exhibition through the untimely loss of their feathers, more particularly those of the tail. This is mainly caused in small yards by their being constantly worried by tyrannical companions; to get away from them the unfortunate bird rushes into corners and out of the way places to escape punishment, and the mischief is done. Every care, then, should be taken to avoid this irreparable loss of plumage by the removal of either the quarrelsome or the unoffending inmate. Again, when handling is necessary for any particular purpose, and a bird of recent introduction evinces a marked dislike to the process, remove it at night from its roosting place, when it will be free from alarm or resistance.

Where selection can be made from a tolerable number of birds, the "matching" of a pen will be greatly facilitated; for this task is another by no means an easy one; a pen of good birds being unnoticed very frequently simply because the exhibitor has, in this respect, lacked the necessary judgment. Where a pair of Houdan hens or pullets are intended to be sent, premising that they are of good size and shape, their heads, crests, and beards should be the counterpart of one another in appearance, and the plumage should also match and be as evenly marked as possible, on the breast particularly, even if the other parts do not so closely correspond, but general evenness of marking should be studiously endeavoured to be maintained, for a "pair" of such birds, correct in every particular of form and feather, are always worth at least three or four times the price of a single bird, owing to their increased usefulness in an exhibitional sense, although the points of the single one may be equivalent in every degree.

In examining and comparing the two hens or pullets, great care must be taken; their legs and plumage should in general correspond as to colour, and their combs, crests, and general form be also similar in size and proportion. Having taken these precautions, a further examination must be passed, as regards the neck-hackles, backs, and tails, which should be of the same colour and marking; the breast and wings must be also carefully examined. Having gone thus carefully through these details, our fancier must endeavour to form some opinion of his own what chance his birds possess of winning. For, whilst insisting on the absolute necessity of a thorough scrutiny on their behalf, and that he should be perfectly cognizant of any shortcoming regarding them, nevertheless, a certain margin may safely be left for what we may term the balance of chances.

Naturally, faults of too prominant a character, cannot be expected to pass muster; but there is this to be said, that even after taking into consideration the now generally acknowledged goodness of show specimens, it yet happens that every point of a bird seldom culminates in absolute perfection. Therefore if the blemishes in the amateur's own birds be of a slight nature only, there is still good hope of winning, inasmuch as few birds (if any) are, as we have aleady intimated, wholly without them; and consequently the imperfections in one pen will be compared with others, thus giving a fair chance to all.

Weight is another thing that must not be overlooked; for the *largest looking* birds are frequently far from the heaviest when placed in the scale, and this item always gains, in this breed, a judge's casting vote, other points being of equal value. To acertain a bird's exact weight in the easiest and readiest manner, the fancier will find the apparatus Fig. 19 invaluable.

The cock must match the females he is to accompany in general appearance, but his comb and wattles should be well developed in contradistinction to these comparatively rudimental appendages in the hens or pullets, and the markings in his case will be a trifle larger in size.

Of recent years "single" classes seem to have been creeping into favour at our large shows, and as many a fancier may have possibly a cock or hen of a really first-class kind, such should be sent in preference to making up an indifferent pen, and thus run the risk of being unnoticed.

The best way for our tyro to follow, when he has decided to exhibit, is to apply to the different secretaries of forthcoming shows for schedules of prizes, in which all particulars connected therewith will be given; he will, as a matter of course, choose the one which appears to him to be the most advantageous and suitable to his birds. When this point is definitely settled and the "entry form," *carefully* filled up, has been forwarded, there will be generally an interval of two or three weeks for final preparation previous to the departure of the birds.

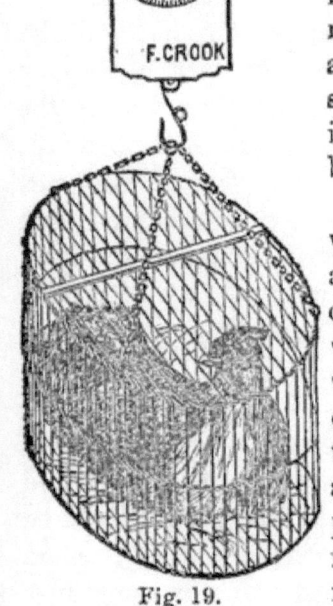

Fig. 19.

Washing, if effected with care, certainly enhances the appearance of the plumage, and the generality of exhibitors make a point of doing it the night before they send their birds off. Regarding the Ordinary variety, the process is not absolutely requisite, if they have had a fair-sized grass run; but it will be found necessary to cleanse their legs with soap and water by means of a tolerably hard nail-brush; and also to wash their combs, wattles, and faces; and their crests in particular will probably require some attention. In the case of the "white" variety, however, washing is more particularly required for the attainment of that almost absolute purity of feather which competition demands, and in fact *necessitates*, in the case of all white birds. Further details on this subject will be found in the short chapter we have devoted to "White Houdans."

To improve the look of the birds, some exhibitors "oil the red," as it is technically termed; that is, with a slightly greased piece of clean rag or sponge they gently rub over the comb and wattles; it certainly gives a very soft, brilliant appearance; but the objection to it is that, if at all *overdone*, the least exposure to dust makes the parts thus anointed look infinitely worse for the operation: diluted vinegar, similarly applied, will give the desired result, without any attendant drawback.

A strong round or oval-shaped hamper is, perhaps, the best for the conveyance of the birds; clean, short straw or hay should be placed at the bottom; a small cabbage and a largish piece of the bottom of a loaf, slightly moistened, both well secured with string to opposite sides of the hamper, should also be provided for them to peck at during their journey; where the latter is of considerable extent, port wine is sometimes given to the birds to make them sleep during the greater part of it. We may add that any damaged feathers, that is to say bent ones, should be carefully removed, and the plumage smoothed in the proper direction with a very soft cloth before the birds are placed in the basket.

"There is much *finesse* in exhibiting," remarks Mr. Long,* "intelligent fanciers necessarily think for themselves, and discover innumerable little wrinkles whereby their stock may be improved and expenses lessened. Birds are usually forwarded "without delay" by the railway, and in most cases they may be left on their runs until within an hour or less of their departure by a train, which may be fixed upon as certain to land them in sufficient time.

"At some shows the rules are so stringent, that five minutes after the stated time a pen would be disqualified, an entry refused or forfeited, or a slight clerical error admitted as an objection to a prize winner. As a rule, these narrow views are adopted by the agricultural shows, where poultry are admitted as the small fry, for the pleasure of the farmer's wife and those towns-folk who are unable to delight in cattle. As examples we know of one case in which a cup, awarded to Brahmas, was withheld through their being accidentally described in the catalogue as Bantams; and in another entries were refused the day after "closing," although four times the amount was offered for each. At all properly organized poultry shows, however, a fair margin is allowed, and an omission in description, age, &c., does not disqualify.

"It is important in some cases where an entry is made in a "variety" class; if the exhibitor keep two or more varieties competent to enter, he is bound to send that entered if he give the exact description, whereas it will be noticed that the leading exhibitors give neither name of variety, or age, in such cases.

"When all is ready, and the train selected, the hamper to which the secretary's printed label has been tied may be dispatched, and perhaps, if a catalogue is sent for, patience

---

* "Poultry for Prizes and Profit." *James Long.*

may be rewarded," although, as the writer judiciously observes, "too much should not be expected at first; and unless the birds are sufficiently good to warrant being "high up," they had better stay at home. Many an amateur has split upon the rock of hope, and swam to shore on the wings of disappointment."

The above remarks are worth remembering, for, as will have been gathered from observations in the Chapter IV., the grand object with the amateur fancier in exhibiting is, that he may judge his birds by comparison, and thus discover from time to time how, and in what manner, he can improve his stock; as his birds improve with his own more matured knowledge, exhibition generally will be found to *decrease* his expenditure by bringing himself, and his birds, more prominently forward; and thus, by creating a market for his eggs and stock, place a very satisfactory balance on the proper side of his " poultry book."

Fowls should on no consideration be sent off to a show with their crops full of hard grain, such a practice being particularly unadvisable; they get hot and feverish, and thus lose condition. Their treatment on their return is frequently of still more importance; and as the feeding even now, at many shows, is guided more by a sense of convenience than by what is really necessitated on the part of the birds, the latter often evince a feverish tendency when they arrive home. If such is apparent, a very moderate repast of *warm* soft food, with very little drink, for the next four and twenty hours, should be given; and by administering to each bird one tea-spoonful of castor oil the last thing at night, and a moderate supply of green food the next morning, they will soon come round. It occasionally happens that fowls are so weakened and exhausted from the cruel practice of *over-showing* that the use of stimulants becomes almost a necessity; port wine, or a pill of barley-meal, well seasoned with pimento, ginger, camphor, or cayenne pepper, are the usual remedies. We need scarcely say that on the part of fowls so invalided, separation from the rest of the stock is necessary.

Although Houdans will stand the fatigue and excitement of showing equally with most breeds, it is painful to witness, as we so frequently have done, these uncomplaining creatures—*un*complaining, be it always recollected, from their utter inability to do otherwise—literally "done to death." Viewing the mere act of exhibition and what it involves, even in its most favorable light,—that is to say when such is really conducted with some due regard to the health and comfort of the birds—the proceeding is not entirely devoid of a certain degree of cruelty, notwithstanding what is said on the contrary. Let any reader picture to himself, if he can, what his own feelings would be, in being placed in a hamper, consigned to the dark recesses of a railway luggage van for several hours; on arriving at his destination, being taken out and confined within the narrow limits of a barred cage, scarcely large enough to admit of his turning about with any moderate degree of ease; to be kept in such a cage for two or three, or even more, days at a stretch, in frequently an oppressive atmosphere; again transferred to the hamper to repeat a similar process perhaps miles hence, and then the final journey home. If any exhibitor can truly realize these conditions, let him reflect upon the feelings of the birds, drooping gradually in their prisons, with no excitement about the honour of winning and anxious only for the termination of their confinement and a return to the open air, grass fields, and liberty; and let us hope, for humanity's sake, he will for the future show some slight compassion on his feathered prisoners, even if it may be to the loss of a money prize or cup.

To the genuine fancier, who is always something of an enthusiast, these remarks in no way apply; for *he* cares for, and really values, his birds, as "pearls above price." It is to that class of exhibitors, who are reckless as to the consequences, *so that they win*—such indeed as we have alluded to in page 88, and to which we more particularly direct our present remarks. The difference between these two classes, it will thus be seen, is considerable; one attaches merely a monetary value to his birds, proportionate with their capabilities, *for the time being*, of fanning the flame of their owner's supposed popularity. The other devotes his time and attention to the pursuit " for the love of it," and when he does carry off a prize, he has the inward satisfaction of feeling that he has *honestly* earned his success. When fanciers of the latter class compete, their birds are certain to be properly looked after, and however hard it may be at times to "lose," if their rivals also exhibit in the same spirit which instigates themselves, their want of success is less keenly felt, for honest rivalry is the very back-bone and essence of poultry-fancying and exhibiting.

In reference to judging, well-proportioned bulk, combined with healthy condition, *should* in our opinion have precedent over most other points in every case where decision wavers, although we may add the rule is seldom observed; the *utility* of the Houdan, rather than its mere ornamentability, we think ought to be considered far oftener than appears to be the case.

It will be seen that we have appended three different scales of points for deciding the relative merits of the breed in the show pen. The first, which was framed by Mr. Tegetmier, is taken from "The English Standard of Excellence," as follows:—

THE HOUDAN FOWL.

Points in Houdans.	
Size	4
Crest	4
Symmetry	2
Plumage	2
Condition	2
Five claws	1
	15

Disqualifications in Houdans.

Absence of crest

Deformity of any kind.

Main colour, or ground colour, any other than Black and White.

Since competition, however, has increased with such gigantic strides, it has been thought that the total number of 15 points, as above given, are for various reasons practically inadequate for arriving at correct decisions; this has induced our Transatlantic cousins to add considerably thereto in framing a standard of their own; in fact, to bring it up to 100 points, as the following schedule from "The American Standard of Excellence" will testify :—

Meritorious points in Houdans.	
Size	25
Crest	15
Breast	10
Comb	10
Symmetry	15
Plumage	15
Condition	10
	100

Disqualifications.

Absence of crest, muffling, and fifth toe, deformity of any description, the ground colour any other than Black and White. Colour not matching in pen. Red feathers in any part of the plumage. Feathers on legs.

The superiority of this scale over the preceding, and the facility with which it carries out the object of its compilers, is very obvious. But as certain differences in value between the sexes, even by this standard, are not provided for, Mr. Wright has shown the propriety of attaching values to *defects* only, rather than to points of merit, which the subjoined table from the "Illustrated Book of Poultry," will readily convey:—

VALUE OF DEFECTS IN JUDGING.

Points of Merit.	*Defects to be Deducted.*	
A bird perfect in shape, carriage, and colour, and in perfect health and condition, to count in points 100	Bad comb	7
	Deficiency in crest or muffling	12
	Straw-coloured feathers	9
	Plumage too light, or to dark, or unevenly broken	8
	Want of size	20
	,, condition	15
	,, symmetry	12

Disqualifiations.— Absence of fifth toe, absence of muffling, of beard, or of crest. Red or brown feathers in plumage, or total absence of black or white. Yellow or feathered shanks. Wry tails, or any other bodily deformity, any fraudulent dying, dressing, or trimming.

We should mention that, in appending the foregoing scales, our object has been rather, to afford the amateur opportunities during his leizure moments, of advantageously studying the points of his birds, and thus forming for himself some accurate opinion of their actual competitive value—than as suggesting on our own part any fixed or arbitrary table for judging them—for this must of necessity be guided, to a great extent, by increased competition as the standard of perfection yet further advances.

CHAPTER VII.

WHITE HOUDANS.

WHITE Houdans, although not so generally known as their more familiar mottled kindred, are nevertheless far from being uncommon, either in England, France, or America, and appear to us to demand a few words entirely to themselves.

This variety shows all the usual characteristics of the breed, excepting colour, which should be pure white. A town yard, however, is certainly *not* best adapted for them, owing to their their plumage becoming soiled so easily, not but what white birds of other breeds have, we know, been not only kept in space of a very limited extent, and under other great disadvantages, which have proved a source of no inconsiderable profit to their owner, beating, in fact, darker colours of the same variety, frequently in the show pen; and we can allude to Cochins in this respect as an example; but this must necessarily be attributed more to the large amount of skill pourtrayed in preparing them for the contest, than to the delicacy of appearance their plumage would otherwise have presented.

Of all the white fowls of the various denominations, each, it would appear, possesses its own ardent admirers; and there seems to be no reason why a white Houdan variety should prove an exception. However well adapted, too, birds of the ordinary marked character may appear on a lawn or well-kept plot of grass, it will be allowed that they must suffer by comparison with any white compatriots as to striking beauty and dignity of appearance. Indeed, what Miss Fairhurst has said of the white Dorkings might, we think, be said with equal justice of this variety, "that their dress of pure white satin, with its red coral ornaments, is a regal court suit, in which they are fit for presentation to their Sovereign any day, on the grassy banks of whose mansion no more lovely ornament could be placed. They are equally to be desired for the country villa, wherever a grass run can be secured in front of the garden, protected by a wire or sunk fence, so that they can be *seen*, along with the flowers, giving life and beauty to the scene."

It has been suggested that the white Houdan has been produced by breeding from the ordinary, but very light-coloured birds, and continuing this selection from season to season until the results have been obtained. But from observations, founded on our actual experience, coupled with the results we have further received from many esteemed correspondents, the white Houdan—unlike the white Dorking to which Mr. Tegetmier has ascribed as being the probable originator of all the other varieties of that breed—is an undoubted *sport* from the ordinary black and white birds. In many cases these "sports" have been bred from at a comparatively recent date with very favourable results, and we are moreover aware that more than one cultivator of the ordinary type of fowl are directing their attention at this very time to the culture of what may eventually prove a popular, pleasing, and no less ornamental addition to the better-known variety.

White Polands must not be confounded with white Houdans, however, which has been done more than once; but any one really possessing the slightest acquaintance with the two respective breeds, the difference we should imagine would soon be apparent. The bluish tinge of leg, faint though it may be in the white Polish, is nevertheless particularly characteristic—to say nothing of the fleshy excrescence of skull, which is more marked in this breed, together with the length of tail and the general bearing, presenting a wide contrast.

The major portion of the earlier specimens were, as a rule, minus the extra toe, which inclines us to believe that in breeding from them a cross with the white Crêve-cœur had very judiciously been employed, but failed simply because a hen of that breed had been introduced instead of a male bird. Latterly we have seen several specimens in which the fifth toe was not only, present but perfectly developed, and the crest and muffling very fairly proportioned; but the birds themselves showed a marked falling off in size. This, too may possibly be accounted for by the present existing small number comparatively of the white breed, necessitating the breeding from very intimately-related blood. If the sphere of its culture, however, be encouraged, as we think it might be by poultry-committees awarding distinct prizes, we certainly believe there is every expectation of seeing quite as high a standard in this respect realized as is already attained in the spangled birds which fanciers are better acquainted with.

To our thinking, the better plan to be pursued to attain size, without injuring the general character in any considerable degree, would be to mate a couple of pure white hens of the largest make obtainable with a perfectly black Crêve cock; by so doing not only a fair proportion of five-clawed chickens might naturally be expected—the hen's influence in this respect being greater than the male bird's—but the desired white plumage would be more probably insured. It may appear strange, and doubtless it is, but it is a well known fact nevertheless that it *is* the black-plumaged birds which so frequently throw the *white* chickens. Indeed, of all changes of colours, a pure white from a jet-black is, perhaps, one of the very easiest to be obtained, and is exemplified in many instances in poultry breeding.*

Like the ordinary variety, the characteristic features of white Houdans should to a great extent assimilate, excepting that the plumage should be of an uniform, pure rich white; but the following points we should like to see cultivated:—The crest in the cock bird to be as profuse as possible, falling gracefully over the sides and the back of the neck, in a semicircular sweep, showing the antlered comb in its fullest proportions and perfection. The brilliant redness of this last-mentioned feature, together with the wattles, which should be thinnish at the edges, and which might, we think, with every advantage to this variety be longer and more pendulous than are usually met with, their greater scope and florid appearance affording a more marked and prettier contrast to the otherwise snowy whiteness of plumage. The whiskers should cover the face to some extent—beak be black; neck nicely curved; body deep and broad; saddle also broad, and corresponding somewhat to the width of the shoulders; a fullish breast; thighs very strongly made, but short; legs tolerably thick, but short also, set well apart, and as white as possible; all the toes, with the exception of the fifth, firm and straight, but the orthodox *fifth* — if it must be retained—should curve with an upward tendency, and be quite distinct from the rest; the tail very full, well sickled,

---

* It is a singular circumstance, that when a variation of colour takes place in the plumage of birds, the change from black to white appears to be much more easily effected than from any other colour to white. Thus, when black-red and white Game fowls are crossed, Piles are produced, in which the black disappears, but the red of the saddle and hackle remains. By crossing a Golden-spangled and white Polish, these spangled buff or Chamois Polish are produced, in which the black spangle of the Golden bird is changed into the white spangle of the Buff, the ground colour remaining almost unchanged.—"The Poultry Book," page 221.

K

and somewhat erect; an upright carriage will enhance that commanding, graceful, and attractive appearance which the Houdan breed so pre-eminently possesses.

The hen should resemble her male companion in contour and carriage; but her crest be as solid-looking and globular in shape as possible, with an antlered comb similar to the cock, but of larger size than in the ordinary variety, and the wattles also, for the reason already given; the beard and muffling full, but distinct; in fact, as in giving our own conception of what a first-class hen ought to be, in page 24, as there described, of a bell-shaped form, and hanging somewhat loosely from the under part of the beak; the beak itself black, as in the cock; a well-arched neck; nice square and deep body; with a fully developed breast; well formed, but short thighs and shanks, white in colour, and tolerably well apart, as in the male bird, so as not to look out of character with the broadness of the body; feet similar; and the tail well carried and moderately proportioned.

Like the generality of white-plumaged fowls, white Houdans appear to prove no exception to the proverbial straw or lemon tint manifesting itself as they mature; but more particularly conspicuous in the neck-hackles, shoulders, and saddle of the cock birds; for neither ourselves or others have apparently noticed it so much in the hens. This should be guarded against, as far as it is practicable, by breeding from specimens as free in this respect as it is possible to procure them. But to infer that a pure rich white is never to be met with in the males, we would not for a moment urge; for a very promising male bird we saw last year—owned by a lady fancier of rising merit—whose plumage betrayed at the completion of his second season scarcely any departure from the white tint so desired.

We have said that town yards are not the most suitable

for white-plumaged birds; but the variety we are discussing appear to be somewhat harder and closer feathered—judging from what we have seen—than the ordinary spangled fowls; and therefore their plumage is less likely to be affected by a smoky atmosphere than that of white birds perhaps usually is.

To keep the plumage in truly white condition, the fowls should not be unnecessarily exposed to the scorching rays of the summer's sun—this, beyond a doubt, influencing the yellowish tinge previously spoken of, and which is so highly objectionable to all white-plumaged birds of the domestic kind. Covered runs are the best preventative, combined with country road-side grit of a very clean description, for them to dust in. Lime has also been recommended as an addition to the dust bath,—its utility in a sanitary sense is evident—but this is, we are convinced, instrumental in producing the very effect it is desired to prevent. More than one individual breeder of white fowls have, we believe, thus cared for, sent their birds to shows, where they have taken the highest honours without any other preparation whatever; but we must admit that all white-plumaged fowls certainly appear to greater advantage by a preparatory washing. In his practical little work,* Mr. J. Long has penned a few brief remarks respecting this operation, which, although so frequently performed, is seldom carried out effectually. He says "White birds may be well washed in a large pan of hot soap suds. The bird should be thoroughly immersed, well lathered with yellow soap, rinsed in cold water—tepid in winter—and placed in a basket of clean straw before a good fire. When we say 'well washed,' we mean it; some persons have an idea that it is necessary only to scrub the bird's legs, and sponge down his hackle, saddle, wings, &c., with a sponge or flannel which has been well

---

* "Management of the Poultry-yard," page 23.

soaped; this is a mistake, as the bird usually looks worse for his cleaning. The bath should be made to the consistency of a wash-woman's 'suds,' and the fowl bodily immersed; let him stand in it during the operation, and when he is well lathered with the soap, the hand may be well rubbed into the 'fluff' passed amongst the feathers of the cushion (if a hen) and well worked over the breast, hocks, &c. Some fanciers use a small, moderately hard brush for the hackle, using it well soaped, and brushed downwards over the feather. In drying, it is well to place the hamper a foot above the ground, that the heat may get under the bird. Even when thoroughly clean, the wet feathers look dirty, and only display their whiteness when yielding to the gentle heat they open out into their normal form."

The undermentioned particulars respecting this variety have been very kindly forwarded by a gentleman whom we may observe is a fancier of great celebrity, but whose name we are not authorised to mention. They probably will be read with some degree of interest, and it is to be regretted that the sequel proved so unfortunate, for the endeavour would appear to have given hopeful promise of far more prosperous results. Our correspondent writes thus:—

"My first experience of white Houdans was amongst a brood of newly-hatched chickens, when I was surprised to observe that one of the little ones presented a marked contrast to the black and whitish-yellow furred appearance of the others, which characterises the Houdan in its incipient stage, for it more closely resembled a canary in colour than any thing else, and I at once concluded that an egg from one of my cross-breds had got mixed with those of my Houdans, and hatched accordingly. Knowing, however, that from the care I had always taken, this could not very well occur I was rather nonplussed. At all events I left it with the others; and, with the rest of the little ones, it grew apace, throwing out a perfectly pure white plumage, and when full-grown certainly presented—at least, to my mind—a particularly novel and attractive appearance, being, in fact, as pretty and tame a pullet as it has ever been my lot to meet with.

"After a time, being ambitious of propagating a white variety if I possibly could, but not succeeding in procuring an entirely white cock—although I searched 'up hill and down dale' in the endeavour—I matched her at last, with as light a coloured cock as I could get, with a full and well-furnished crest, &c., which accorded well in this respect with the pullet, but in other details he was only moderate. From this union, every egg produced I carefully saved; but the first batch set were every one spoilt through the vacillating disposition of a borrowed hen. The next lot hatched out very well, but I looked in vain for any canary-coloured chickens, such as I had been anticipating, all turning out ordinary-marked youngsters. However, I didn't despair, and in the next batch I was at length rewarded by *two* out of eight chicks, showing the future indications of being *quite* white, nor was I disappointed. But sad to relate, before my 'spotless' beauties were of 'marriageable' age, I lost my white hen from misdirected kindness, I verily believe on my part, by over-feeding; for, as I have said, she was a particularly tame bird, and I seldom went into the yard without throwing her something.

"My hopes now rested on the two pullets, which certainly promised to equal their departed parent; and being really very good in most points, at the instigation of my old friend Mr. B—, I was induced to enter them at a forthcoming show. The night previously, I washed them well, put them in a hamper nicely littered with short straw—and strictly according to the instructions for poultry exhibition—placed them before the fire to dry. I really think that I was that night more solicitous about the birds in the basket than I was about anything else in my life. Before I retired to rest I removed them, looking, to my eye, marvellously well, still in their basket, to a nice warm out-house, and engaged a man to call early in the morning to take them to the neighbouring railway station, whence they were to make their first journey in what I fondly fancied would be an eventful career. I dreamt that night that I had founded a new colony with my white birds. In the morning I awoke before my usual time; the excitement—it is, perhaps, foolish to admit it—would not suffer me to sleep, and the musings at early dawn were really a prolongation of my dreams. It is not without a certain amount of grim humour that I now record the sad termination of them:—

"I was impatient to get at my birds, and start them on their journey—so impatient that before I had barely finished my dress, I sent the servant for the baskets. Presently I heard cries of 'Oh! sir! please, sir! come out directly!'— I did'nt know what to think; I hurried out, with only one boot on, and the whole weight of cruel disappointment and blighted ambition then fell upon me—a certain indescribable confusion in the yard,—the open door,—the basket turned over,—some scattered white feathers, and disturbance of the gravel outside, revealed the catastrophe too plainly to me. Some brutal surburban thief had entered my yard, and carried off my hopes;—alas! too plainly I saw it—with some four other birds. I could—as bereaved folks sometimes say—have foregone all the others, if my *two* had only been spared me. I hastily summoned the local policeman; he found the thief's footprints, told me how he had got in, and how he had got out; he reported the case, called again upon me, but brought me no tidings of the thief, whose evil steps were on that fatal night directed but too successfully to the shed where I had unhappily placed my promising white birds. I have got over it now; but failing to meet with any more white pullets good enough for my purpose, I have since confined myself to the breeding of the old variety, but if a favourable chance presents itself, I shall again turn my attention in the former direction, feeling convinced that the white variety will sooner or later make a rare name for themselves."

Respecting our correspondent's concluding remarks, there no doubt *is* a wide field opened for persevering breeders in this direction; for it appears to us that a few seasons devoted to the proper selection and breeding of this ornamental class would make a very ample return for the trouble expended. But success can only be obtained by carefully watching each new development, and making use of every ascertained fact in breeding; or, in other words, by strictly following out everything which gives promise of satisfactory results. We, can however, frame no golden rule for achieving immediate success. In addition to what we have previously suggested, we might perhaps advise that, as good white specimens as can possibly be secured should hold precedence, in point of mating, and that all birds which have already thrown white offspring should also be bred from largely. From such, one or two chickens almost for a certainty would make themselves conspicuous in this desired feature, although the majority would naturally revert to the ordinary spangled type. But by mating the few chickens thus produced with others also of white plumage, the chickens in the next generation, may fairly be expected to show this desired feature in greater numbers; and by further care and attention in the same direction, a characterized white plumage would, with time, become thoroughly established.

Like their mottled-plumaged brethren, it is worth remarking that white Houdans appear to feather and grow equally fast, are quite as hardy, and to rival them in their egg-productive faculties.

As the white variety is as yet but comparatively in its infancy, our presumption will doubtless be questioned for attempting to frame a standard for judging it. But as we hope soon to see it come to the front in formidable array, we have ventured to construct a scale based upon Mr. Wright's system—and as already given by him for estimating the show value of the ordinary variety.

SCALE FOR JUDGING WHITE HOUDANS.

Meritorious Points.	*Imperfections to be deducted.*	
A bird perfect in size, shape, style, condition, &c., and of good colour, to reckon in points ... 100	Smallness of crest or muffling.	12
	Faulty comb	8
	Bad colour	14
	Crooked breast...	16
	Want of size	20
	" Symmetry	12
	" Condition	15

Disqualifications.—Wry-tails, absence of the fifth toe, or muffling, beard or crest, any coloured feathers in plumage. Legs any other colour but white, or pinkish white, or having any signs of feathers. Any fraudulent dressing, colouring, or trimming of either combs or plumage.

Although the real utility of the above scale can be determined only by actual test, we nevertheless venture to think that it will be found to approximate, more or less correctly, to that which hereafter possibly will prove, on trial, the best adapted. But what we have already said respecting the previous standards applies with equal consistency to this—viz., that in appending one and all of them, we have done so really with the view of assisting the amateur—and which we believe they will do in a very great measure—by enabling him to arrive at a tolerably correct idea of the true show value of the birds rather than by framing any fixed scale, which, after all, must of necessity be more or less empirical.

WALTER HAWKINS, Printer, 3, Albert Terrace, Paddington, W.

www.ingramcontent.com/pod-product-compliance
Lightning Source LLC
Chambersburg PA
CBHW030342170426
43202CB00010B/1216